The History of Data Storage

From Cathode Ray Tubes to Resistive RAM

*

By Larry Freeman

If you would not be forgotten as soon as you are dead and rotten, either write something worth reading or do things worth the writing.

–Benjamin Franklin

***

Table of Contents

***

Welcome to *The History of Data Storage*!

In 2010, as I was completing the book "The Evolution of the Storage Brain" I wrote that we were on the cusp of some important innovations that would fundamentally change how digital information would be stored and retrieved. To say that much has changed since that book would be an understatement. For instance:

- Solid state devices have infiltrated nearly every aspect of storage architecture, and will be the dominant storage medium of the future.
- Other technologies that were just emerging in 2010 - notably cloud computing and cloud storage - have now matured and appear poised for widespread adoption.
- New technologies and storage constructs have emerged that were not even recognized in 2010. These concepts, such as Big Data and the Software-Defined Data Center (SDDC), while admittedly still in an experimental phase, are showing great promise.

This updated book covers the underpinnings and evolution of digital data storage over the past 70-odd years, since the post-WWII discovery of commercial computing. In this book, you'll see some new predictions as well as a review of some of my prior predictions. If you are familiar with my earlier book, you'll notice some restructuring of chapters as well as the addition of a few new ones. For instance, some new chapters will offer more depth on the emerging importance of three new technology trends: flash memory, cloud storage and scale out storage.

And, for those who think that technology (especially data storage technology) can be boring at times, I'd like to refer you to this book's four-part epilogue, "Deceit, Theft, Espionage, and Murder in the Storage Industry." After reading this section, you'll realize that our industry has not been immune from the foibles of human nature.

So sit back, relax, and enjoy reading about the latest trends and evolving technologies that allow us to store, serve, and protect the vital information necessary in our data-driven society.

Larry Freeman
storagebrain@gmail.com

Introduction

When compared with today's compact mobile devices, it's hard to imagine how much space it used to take to store 5 MB of data. The above image[1] offers one glimpse. It shows what it took in 1956 to transport 5MB of storage (and very large disk platters). According to one source,[2] such systems weighed more than a ton and had to be transported via forklift and cargo plane. Talk about a forklift upgrade!

***

From Primitive Storage to Advanced Intelligence

Today's data storage systems are a lot like the human brain. They are both capable of storing valuable information. They are both critical to the successful operation of their "network" of moving parts. Each has discrete components that must work synergistically with other elements in order to achieve true intelligence. In both the human brain and the data storage "brain," higher level intelligence has evolved from largely primitive origins.

> **Bits & Bytes:** Did you know that the average human brain is capable of storing the equivalent of 2.5 petabytes of information?[3]

In the upcoming chapters of this book, I'll be describing how the various components used to build a data storage system have evolved to their current state.

From the not-so-distant past to the present, readers of this book will take what I hope will be an entertaining and enlightening expedition that will eventually conclude several years in the future, as I unveil what "storage system intelligence" might look like in another 10 or 20 years' time.

Why Should You Care?

Why join me in this excursion? Since you're reading this, I'll assume you already have some interest in data storage. My guess is you may be an enterprise IT or storage architect, storage administrator, or an IT manager or director involved in some aspect of your organization's enterprise data storage needs.

You may be a CIO or CTO, and for you this book might be of particular interest. You are the person that your organization depends upon to cut through the myriad of choices and decide on the most appropriate technologies to run your business. Making the wrong technology choices can have disastrous results for you and those that trust your decisions.

Understanding the history of a particular segment of technology — in this case data storage technology — and the reasons for its transitions will prepare you for today's decisions and tomorrow's breakthroughs.

Regardless of your job title or your reasons for reading this book, today many of us are consumed with solving today's most pressing, day-to-day issues. Because of that, it's often difficult to take time and just sit and think about where our industry has been — and where it could go.

However, I believe the knowledge you'll gain in doing this will help you understand how the data storage industry arrived at the juncture we see today, and will be invaluable in helping you position yourself and your organization to benefit most from what data storage has to offer today, as well as what's in store for the future.

As Aristotle once said, *"If you would understand anything, observe its beginning and its development."* So, let's get ready - and begin our own journey of understanding.

Some of the Places We'll Go

Here are just a few of the areas we'll address:

- The history of disk drives: A cautionary tale of consolidation
- When it all goes wrong: disk drive failures and data corruption
- The storage brain - internal and external components

- Advanced intelligence, virtualization, and scale out
- Cloud and flash – moving from hype to hyper-adoption

Who You'll Be Traveling With

I've appointed myself your tour guide of sorts, on this journey into the past, present and future of data storage. For those who don't know me, let me tell you something about myself and the inspiration behind this book:

- **Who I am:** I entered the data storage industry in 1979. Since then, believe me, I've seen a lot of changes in the technologies used to store and retrieve data. Over the years, I've held positions with various data storage companies in engineering, sales, product marketing, business development, and corporate strategy. Some of the companies I've worked for include Data General, Telex Computer Products, NEC Information Systems, Spectra Logic, and NetApp.

  As you can probably tell, I love to speak and write about data storage. I have always had an inquisitive mind, and I enjoy sharing what I've learned with others. From the beginning, I noticed that data storage technologies were traveling at a very fast pace, but no one was documenting these advances in a way that put all the puzzle pieces together. Being fortunate enough to have spent nearly 40 years watching this industry grow, I decided that I would take on this task.

About this Book and its Contributors

This book is primarily based on my observations of the evolution of data storage during my time in the industry: From primitive, slow standalone disk drives (where reliability was usually measured in hundreds of hours!) -- to today's highly intelligent, lightning-fast disk arrays that are virtually indestructible. Along with my own thoughts, this book is the collaborative result of many others as well, such as:

- **Third-Party Sources:** Where possible, I've included references to interesting articles, books or presentations that shed further light on a specific comment I make. For those of you interested in doing further research, I encourage you to peruse the links and resources referenced in each chapter's endnotes.

- **NetApp Experts.** I have included the perspective of several experts I worked with during my 10 years at NetApp. These were trusted resources I relied upon on during my tenure there. They also represent some of the sharpest storage industry scientists, architects, and designers I've yet to come across.

The Quest for Perfect Storage

In the beginning of this section, I used an analogy that the storage brain was much like the human brain. I'd like to take this idea one step further for a moment and delve into the area of brain function.

When either the human brain (or its data storage counterpart) doesn't operate at or above par, it can cause great consternation — especially when you depend on it to perform increasingly complex tasks. Alternately, if the human or data storage brain successfully demonstrates higher level functioning and advanced efficiency, it can be the source of great power and achievement.

In an IT organization's efforts to move away from the first, negative outcome and closer to the second, positive one, a picture begins to emerge regarding what might be considered the future, "perfect" storage brain.

As we highlight the history and future of storage intelligence, Table 1 might help. This table offers some of the storage brain's evolving characteristics that will be important to keep in mind.

Table 1. Attributes of the Perfect Brain.

Desirable Characteristics	
The Human Brain	The Data Storage Brain
• High I.Q.	• Highly advanced system intelligence
• Fast at learning new tasks and retaining new information	• Store and retrieve data quickly with minimal data latency
• Perform well under pressure, recover from illness or injury	• Perform well, even when faced with high data I/O demand or component failure
• Complete tasks with minimal effort and energy	• Maximize the utilization of disk space, minimize the power needed to operate
• Quickly become "unconsciously competent" at routine tasks	• Perform routine tasks automatically, with minimal management oversight
• Benefit from investment in higher learning	• Improved intelligence and performance via hardware and software upgrades

Storage . . . along the Space-Time Continuum

When I think of the evolution of data storage intelligence, I tend to categorize it within four distinct eras, as shown in Table 2. Again, using the analogy of human brain development, a correlation can be made to the development of data storage intelligence.

Table 2. The Four Eras of Data Storage Design.

Era 1: Reliant (1951-1970)	Era 2: Dependent (1971-1990)	Era 3: Independent (1991-2010)	Era 4: Mature (2011+)
Storage is:	*Storage is:*	*Storage is:*	*Storage is:*
Monolithic	Distributed	Virtualized	Abstract
Expensive	Affordable	Efficient	Enlightened
Mainframe-attached	Server-attached	Network-attached	Cloud-attached
Compute-centric	OS-centric	Application-centric	Data-centric

...And How Each Era Corresponds to a Stage in Human Development...

Infancy	*Childhood*	*Adolescence*	*Adulthood*

The above chart depicts a general trend from the early days of dumb, monolithic storage systems to today's modern equivalent: Modular and increasingly intelligent networked storage systems now in use along a cross-section of industries.

Reaching Full Maturity: The Future of Data Storage

In this introduction, we've seen the data storage brain "evolve" from infancy through adolescence to adulthood. Today, in this adult brain, serious thinking has begun to occur. Data storage will move into a future where it will benefit from the history and wisdom gained thus far.

For now, as I look ahead into my storage crystal ball (and seek opinions of my fellow soothsayers), let me leave you with just a few questions to be answered regarding the future of data storage into the year 2020, and beyond.

We'll delve into each of these later in more detail:

- Solid state devices will play an increasingly larger role in tomorrow's data center, but will they ever truly replace the world of spinning disk?
- Cloud storage is an inescapable conclusion, but what form will it most likely take in your organization?
- Storage systems will exhibit more advanced forms of intelligence, especially in the areas of agility and efficiency. What are these emerging technologies and how do they fit in today's IT infrastructure?
- Advanced storage management features are on the horizon. Will they make quicker work for administrators?

Join me as we explore each of these areas in the coming chapters.

Endnotes Referenced in Introduction

1 "A Look Back: 5MB Hard Disk from 1956," TechEBlog, April 12, 2007,
   http://www.techeblog.com/index.php/tech-gadget/a-look-back-5mb-hard-disk-
   from-1956.
2 "Talking Tech," by Lee Gomes, The Wall Street Journal, August 22, 2006,
   http://online.wsj.com/.
3 "What is the Memory Capacity of the Human Brain?" by Paul Reber, April 19,
   2010, Scientific American,
   http://www.scientificamerican.com/article.cfm?id=what-is-the-memory-capacity.

Chapter One: And Then There Was Disk...

The foreground of the above photo[4] shows the first commercial disk drive introduced to the world: The IBM 350 storage unit. IBM introduced the 350 in 1956 as part of the company's early RAMAC 305 computer system. (Two 350s are in the photo foreground, with the 305 in the background.). The 350 weighed over a ton, could transfer data at 8800 characters per second, and had fifty 24-inch disk platters capable of spinning at 1200 RPM. It was able to store the equivalent of 4.4MB of data.

* * *

Disk: Still Spinning After 60 Years

There are few mechanical designs that withstand the test of time relatively unchanged. The internal combustion engine is one of them. In the world of storage, it's undoubtedly the design of the basic magnetic hard disk drive (HDD).

Since they first came to market in the late '50s, hard disk drives have relied on the following core components:

- **Heads:** These are 'read/write' heads that use electrical impulses to store (or 'write') and retrieve (or 'read') magnetically recorded bits of data.
- **Platters:** These are magnetically coated disk platters that spin and house these bits of data (similar to an old vinyl record in a record player).
- **Arms:** These are mechanical actuator arms that move the heads back and forth across the spinning disk platters. These, in turn, form concentric 'tracks' of recorded data.

From this basic design have come some great innovations.

The Past: Disk Drives Prior to 1985

The title page of this chapter shows one of the earliest commercial magnetic disk drives. The 350 storage unit would ultimately become just one of many early disk drive inventions by IBM.

The 350 was to be followed by several other models, including:

- The aerodynamic "flying heads" innovation of IBM's 1301 disk storage unit (in 1961)
- The well-known IBM 3340 Direct Access Storage Facility (code-named *Winchester*) in 1973.

For the first time, the Winchester would no longer require interim head unloading from the spinning disk media, a factor that would greatly improve reliability.

> **Behind the "Winchester" Label:** Modern-day magnetic disk drives are still often referred to as Winchester technology. This was the codename coined by IBM's Ken Haughton for the IBM 3340 during its development. Since early 3340 design assumed two 30-megabyte modules in the drive, Haughton associated it with the popular Winchester .30-30 hunting rifle designed by John Browning in 1894. Although the commercial 3340 ended up with different module sizes, the Winchester name still stuck.

For their first 30 years, disk drives exhibited the following characteristics:

- They existed as purely a necessary component in a larger, proprietary mainframe or minicomputer system.
- They were not available separately from other vendors.
- They were very expensive.
- They performed only the most basic of storage functions: Spinning, seeking, reading and writing.
- All their intelligence, relatively speaking, came from a storage control unit.

These early drives were typically called Single Large Expensive Disks (SLEDs). SLEDs ultimately became a dying breed. IBM released the last of its kind in 1989 with the introduction of its IBM 3390 Direct Access Storage Device (DASD).

The Early Days of Disk Drive Communications

In the first several years of disk drive development, all the intelligence and early communication between mainframes and their attached disk storage, relatively speaking, came from a control unit, or controller.

Early communication between the controller and its attached disk storage were based on a few iterations:

- Bus and Tag systems
- Storage Module Device (SMD) Disk Drives

Bus and Tag Systems

With Bus and Tag systems, the controller was typically a refrigerator-sized unit attached to the computer's main CPU.

Early disk storage "channel" controllers in IBM's mainframe environments connected disk or tape storage *control units* to the system via parallel communication channels. These were known as "selector channels."[5] Disk control units were daisy-chained together to the controller via two very large cables. This early cabling was called Bus-and-Tag cabling. Connected disk storage was, thus, often referred to as "channel-attached."

The Bus cable would carry data between the controller and its disk control unit(s), while the Tag cable carried communication protocols (primarily the mainframe block-based multiplex channel protocol).

> **Bits & Bytes:** Old-timers know that the term "pulling cables" in the data center harks back to the age of connecting computers and peripheral devices with heavy Bus-and-Tag cabling systems. Incidentally, the need to daisy-chain so many storage peripherals together with these types of cables heavily influenced the use of raised data center floors in early data center design, so that cables could be buried under the floor.

SMD Disk Drives

As minicomputers came to market and began to diversify the mainframe market, another disk communications protocol emerged: Storage module device (SMD) disk drives. Control Data Corporation first shipped its minicomputer with SMD drives in late 1973.

Somewhat similar to the Bus and Tag cabling system, the SMD interface used much smaller "A" and "B" flat cables to transfer control instructions and data between disk drives, the controller and the computer. Control instructions would pass from the "A" cable while data passed from the "B" cable.[6]

Instead of a control unit, the disk controller shrank down to a single board which was inserted into the system's CPU card cage.

By the late '70s and early '80s, the CDC family's SMD protocol had become widely adopted and used by a variety of disk drive manufacturers who offered both removable and non-removable SMD disk drives. SMD drives were widely OEMed to minicomputer companies by just a few vendors, like CDC, Hitachi, NEC and Fujitsu.

Disk Drives in the '80s and '90s

Disk drives in the late '80s and '90s went through a number of significant transformations that allowed them to be widely used in the emerging open systems world of servers and personal computers. These included:

- The replacement of large 19" disk drives by smaller, less expensive 5.25" (and, eventually, 3.5" and 2.5") drives.

- Advances associated with **redundant arrays of independent disks (RAID)** technology. RAID suddenly allowed smaller, 'cheap' drives to be used on more costly computer systems. *(We'll delve more into RAID and other types of disk drive protection in the next chapter.)*

- The development and widespread adoption of the **Small Computer Systems Interface (SCSI)**. SCSI is a disk system interface that brought further intelligence to I/O buses. SCSI—now in its latest SCSI-3 incarnation—would ultimately define the various ways disk systems connected and communicated with the host via a new type of disk controller known as a host bus adapter (HBA).

'**Scuzzy' or 'Sexy'?** Today, the SCSI interface is widely pronounced as "skuzzy." But, that wasn't always the preferred pronunciation. Larry Boucher (an early Shugart SCSI pioneer who later founded Adaptec) lobbied for the term to be pronounced "sexy" instead.[7] Unfortunately, he lost the battle. (Who said storage isn't sexy, anyways?)

The SCSI Equation

SCSI was a significant breakthrough for disk drives. The interface's main benefit was that it added intelligence to the disk device which could subsequently be leveraged by the storage controller, or Host Bus Adapter (HBA).

Originally designed to be used for all computer peripherals (like today's USB interface) SCSI eventually settled on storage devices and became the de facto industry standard for disk storage.

Disk drives produced today fall into four basic categories, as determined by their cable connections:

- SCSI
- Fibre Channel
- Serial ATA (SATA)
- Serial Attached SCSI (SAS)

Yet, regardless of the category, all are still based on SCSI's Common Command Set (CCS).

Unlike prior interfaces like the Bus and Tag system, SCSI used a single data cable to present its CCS interface with built-in intelligence. This intelligence no longer required the storage controller to send discrete, manual signals to the disk device.

The earlier Bus and Tag interface system was unintelligent and required you to step through the entire process of seeking, retrieving and storing data.

In contrast, the SCSI interface was able to add intelligence to the disk storage device itself.

Now, the SCSI HBA could connect to a device, send commands or ask for status, and simply wait for the device to respond. Up to seven devices could be attached to a single HBA (this would later expand to 15). Device requests could also be queued in an orderly fashion, which greatly improved the efficiency of storing and retrieving data.

SASI, SCSI and the Path to Interoperability

Despite its current widespread use, the road to SCSI adoption was not without hiccups. Originally offered in 1979 by Al Shugart's Shugart Associates, the early interface was known as SASI (for Shugart Associates Systems Interface). In 1981, NEC joined forced with Shugart to submit SASI as a potential standard to the ANSI committee handling I/O standards.

Wanting a more vendor-neutral protocol, ANSI ultimately renamed the standard to SCSI (Small Computer Systems Interface). Although ANSI released the first SCSI standard (now known as SCSI-1) in 1986, it would take several years before many of its early compatibility issues could be resolved.

This was due to the fact that disk drive vendors had developed different interpretations of the early Common Command Set. The SCSI CCS originally contained only a handful of mandatory commands, but had about 100 optional commands that vendors could choose to implement or not.

This led to a very rocky start for the standard. SCSI drives and HBAs from different vendors couldn't communicate with each other since vendors were prone to use the optional commands in different ways.

But, these issues ultimately worked themselves out. ANSI continued to develop a more standardized SCSI Common Command Set. This resulted in today's incarnation, now referred to as SCSI-3.

Today: Disk Drives, Pork Bellies & Price Tags

Over the course of the past few decades, today's crop of magnetic disk storage has made amazing leaps in capacity, reliability and performance. It's also had just as dramatic reductions in both form factor and price.

Disk drive capacity growth has to be one of the most amazing trends in the evolution of data storage. Comparing the early IBM 5MB disk drive to today's ground-breaking 10TB models represents an astounding 2 million-times increase in single drive storage capacity, with physical properties shrinking from thousands on pounds to a few dozen ounces.

Much like pork bellies are traded as a common futures commodity according to supply and demand, basic disk drives have become mere commodities. The vendor playing field has also gone from its heyday of roughly 200 manufacturers to today's HDD industry duopoly of Seagate and Western Digital.[8]

The Paradox of Disk Storage

Today's high capacity, low cost disk drives can be paradoxical to some. How is it that someone can walk into a local retailer and pick up a multi-terabyte disk drive for under a hundred bucks, but when that same drive is placed into an enterprise storage system, the price of the disk drive suddenly becomes thousands of dollars?

Software and Added Intelligence

The answer has to do with the surrounding software intelligence, supporting features and overall system design in enterprise storage. This is what separates today's modern enterprise storage system from a basic, off-the-shelf disk drive.

Conventional wisdom has always been that instead of just cabling together a bunch of 'cheap' disks and hooking them up to application servers, today's enterprise storage system consists of so much more.

Why Pay More?

Recently, however, the entire notion of these semi proprietary enterprise storage systems has been challenged and there is an upsurge of companies that have defied conventional wisdom by offering products with "cheap" storage devices with a new class of products known as "Software-defined Storage", or SDS. We'll learn more about this technology in the upcoming chapter *The Era of Scale*.

Are Disk Drives in Our Future?

As new storage technologies emerge, you will hear predictions about the ultimate demise of the magnetic disk drive. However, this industry's longevity, on-going advances and winning 60-year track record have up until now proved the "disk-is-dead" pundits wrong.

Today's battle cry is that solid state disks (SSDs) will completely replace magnetic disk storage. While solid state disk holds amazing promise, many industry commentators—myself included—don't hold to the prognosis that magnetic disk will ever completely disappear.

(Warning: Geek Alert!) Breaking the Super paramagnetic Limit

Hitting the Capacity Ceiling? The super paramagnetic limit (somewhere between 100-200 gigabits of recording density per square inch) was once thought to be the ceiling for magnetic disk drive capacities.

If you attempted to shrink the disk's ferromagnetic particles (which record the data bits) much smaller than the above limit, you risked the magnetization suddenly "flipping" when reading or writing to disk. This would make the disk unstable and unable to reliably store data.

Today, emerging technologies go far beyond the limits once deemed impenetrable. In fact, today's technologies make it possible to store close to a terabit per square inch of data, with no end in sight. Research into the area of higher capacities for magnetic disk drives is intriguing and fairly exhaustive. I'll mention just a few promising areas:

- **Perpendicular Magnetic Recording (PMR).**
  As opposed to just spanning the surface (or longitude) of the disk platter, perpendicular recording technology penetrates deeper into the disk platter's magnetic surface, a factor that dramatically increases the disk's areal density. Using PMR technology alone, disk drive vendors have, (within the past few years) brought single drive capacities from 2TB to the 4TB level.

- **Helium-Filled Drives.**
  One problem that drive makers have always had to deal with is air turbulence. The speedy spinning motion of the platters disrupts the read/write head's ability to remain on track. Known as track misregistration (TMR), this aerodynamic problem is exacerbated as recording tracks are pushed closer together.

  One drive maker (Hitachi GST, a Western Digital division) produced a helium-filled disk drive that helped solve this problem. Smoother aerodynamics allowed for smaller, tighter recording tracks, and also allowed the disk platters, themselves, to be made thinner. This lead to more disk platters per disk drive and the end result: A near-doubling of single drive capacities.

- **Shingled Magnetic Recording (SMR).**
  When writing data onto a disk platter, electrical energy passes through the write head to magnetize bits on the recording track. When *reading* data from a recorded track, however, only the center portion of the original recorded track is used.

  Since reading the data bits require only a portion of the recording track, the tracks are able to be overlapped (or "shingled"). Drive vendors are now implementing the use of shingled magnetic recording (SMR) as a way to increase single drive capacity by another 1.5-2.5 times.

- **Heat-Activated Magnetic Recording (HAMR).**
  HAMR technology relies on first heating the media so that it can store smaller bits of data per square inch. Scientists claim that this technology holds promise for terabit-per-square-inch recording in the future.

- **Patterned-Bit Recording.**
  Nanotechnologies like patterned-bit recording attempt to shrink data bits down to the size of a few atoms. This technology aligns microscopic grains of magnetic material into well-behaved rows and columns. Using individual grains to record data, it allows for extremely high recording densities.

Looking into the Crystal Ball...

So will disk drives still be around in another 10 or 20 years? And if so, what will they look like?

The End of Disk Drives?

I believe disk drives will very much still be around through 2030 and beyond. They will also look much the same as they do today, but with much higher capacities.

Seagate has promised a 60TB disk drive by 2020, based solely upon using HAMR technology. Combining HAMR with the other technologies mentioned above, disk drives of 100TB or greater are conceivable.[9]

Hybrids in the Era of Intelligent Data Caching

Although HDDs will continue to exist for quite some time, a new breed of drive has emerged: Solid State Drives (or, SSDs). Comprised solely of memory chips, enterprise data storage vendors have embraced the concept of using SSDs in hybrid SSD/HDD data storage system designs. In effect, these hybrid systems mix performance-based solid state memory devices with their capacity-based, traditional, HDD counterparts.

(Don't worry. I've devoted another entire chapter to the evolution of SSDs and other solid state memory technologies.)

This functionality—combining high SSD performance and high HDD disk capacities—makes it feasible to separate hot and cold data by device (SSD for "hot" data, HDD for "colder" data, for instance). This will also make it viable to "spin down" HDDs, except for occasional data updates.

> **Picture This:** A single-rack multi-petabyte storage system filled with about a hundred hybrid devices. Lights are blinking feverishly but no sound is emitted except for the cooling fans and the occasional spin up/spin down of an individual disk drive. In this environment, power and cooling requirements would be a fraction of what they are today, with storage costs reduced to pennies per gigabyte. That, many believe, defines the storage system of the future.

Endnotes Referenced in Chapter 1

4   http://en.wikipedia.org/wiki/Early_IBM_disk_storage.
5   http://en.wikipedia.org/wiki/IBM_System/360.
6   http://en.wikipedia.org/wiki/Storage_Module_Device.
7   From the article "Q&A with Larry Boucher," Smart Computing, January 2002.
8   http://seekingalpha.com/article/3827746-seagate-western-digital-soon-true-
     duopoly-hdds
9   http://www.extremetech.com/computing/122921-seagate-hits-1-terabit-per-
     square-inch-60tb-drives-on-their-way.

Chapter Two: Oh @#$%!

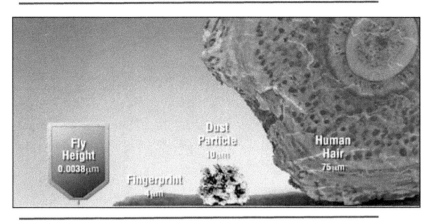

The use of removable platters in early disk drives exacerbated disk failure issues. Platters were stored and transported in 'hat box' containers when not mounted in the drive, and subjected to dust and smoke contamination. Low disk read/write head 'fly heights' were another issue. As shown in this image, even a speck of dust or a human hair could have a catastrophic result. Low fly heights–coupled with less-than-precise air filtering—caused frequent head crashes and data loss. Although much less of a problem today, catastrophic hardware failures such as head crashes are still a concern.

* * *

Coping with Failure

Before you start thinking the above title will send you to some Wayne Dyer self-help e-book, I want to reassure you we are still very much in the land of data storage.

In the last chapter, we discussed advances in the evolution of magnetic disk storage. We also alluded to the fact that disk storage had become more reliable as the years passed and competition increased.

While the above statements are true, I did gloss over one harsh reality about the use of disk storage: Since they are comprised primarily of moving mechanical parts, disk drives are unfortunately prone to failure. In other words, they can crash and/or return errors significant enough to destroy your data (and ruin your day).

> **Watch out! SSD crash ahead.** Although solid state drives (SSDs) contain no moving parts, they are still not immune from crashing. They just crash in a different way. We discuss this further in the chapter devoted to SSDs and solid state memory technologies.

I spent part of my early life as a field engineer routinely telling users that the one thing you can always depend on when you buy a disk drive is that it's going to crash at some point. In fact, if Benjamin Franklin had lived in the time of disk drives, he even might have ended his famous quote differently:

> "In this world nothing can be said to be certain, except death and taxes *[and the likelihood of drive failure]*."

Sorry, Ben. Maybe that *is* going a bit far. . . But, you get the picture.

To its credit, the storage industry ultimately responded to the prospect of disk failure with vast

improvements in mechanical design and some pretty
sophisticated forms of surrounding intelligence. Disk
drives today do an excellent job of overcoming the
inherent risk of failure, but have not completely removed
the risk. Outside of disk failure, there are also other
gremlins that can stand between you and your data. We'll
be discussing a few of those in the next two chapters.
We'll also peer into the future and make some predictions
surrounding protection against both disk drive failure
and other forms of data loss.

Protection: A Necessary Step in Storage Evolution

The last chapter introduced disk as one of the earliest
building blocks in today's storage systems. As more
organizations began depending on disk storage for their
critical applications and data, however, safeguarding disk
systems against the risk of failure and data loss became
another critical evolutionary step.

The Past: Protecting SLEDs

In the early days of disk drives and single large
expensive disk (SLED), head crashes were common. Tape
drives were actually considered much more reliable than
disk. (The opposite is true today, however.)

In those days, disk drives were so expensive that only
a single copy of data was stored online. When a drive
crashed (*when* being the operative word), data was
recovered from a tape copy and restored back to a new
disk. Whole rooms were typically reserved to store the
reel-based backup tapes.

From the 50s until the late 80s, this was the model for
disk drive protection.

Repairing these early disk drives was not for the faint of heart. Powerful drive motors turning heavy disk platters, large, voice coils moving read/write heads back and forth, and relays turning these things on and off often evoked harrowing experiences, two of which I experienced first-hand.

Figure 2-1. Someone Servicing Early Disk Drives.

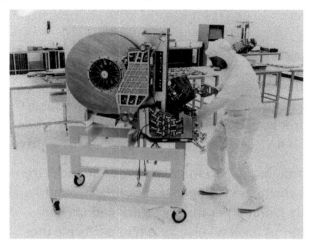

My Early Experiences with Disk Drive Repair...

When adjusting servo tracking systems on early drives, I was always cautioned to disable the emergency retract function for the voice coil by hitting a small switch on the diagnostic tester before I made any adjustments. (Stories of broken fingers and hands for those who forgot this step were usually told with amusement.)

Being in a rush one day I forgot this important detail. Luckily, no broken bones resulted. However, the alignment tool I was holding was snatched from my grasp and vanished into thin air. After much searching, the tool was discovered. It was stuck squarely into a ceiling tile like a well-placed projectile.

Spindle drive motors on early drives demanded a lot of electrical current. Because of this, they were connected to 240-volt, high-amp circuits. One day, going about my business of installing a bank of disk drives, a blinding blue flash of light suddenly passed before me. At the same time, the lights in the data center went out and things became eerily quiet, with one exception: A loud thud that came from the main circuit breaker panel. It was a frightening experience to say the least!

Once I was able to collect my wits and investigate what happened, I discovered an electrician had reversed the hot and ground wires on the 240volt AC receptacle into which I plugged the drive. I nearly became a human lightning rod that day.

RAID in the '80s

A confluence of events in the late '80s would ultimately pave the way for a much more affordable disk storage paradigm. It also led to a significant reduction in the risk of data loss due to failure of a single disk drive.

California-based Sun Microsystems advanced the concept of client/server "open computing" systems and was quickly gaining popularity. Workstations and personal computers had also begun to permeate the enterprise and academic institutions.

At around this time, an enterprising team of scientists at the University of California, Berkeley, began to postulate a way to boost data I/O in order to keep up with the faster RISC processors that were powering these new servers. The team's ideas ultimately made their way into a now-famous 1987 paper[10] called, *"A Case for Redundant Arrays of Inexpensive Disks."* RAID was born. A few of the ideas promoted included:

- The use of a group of smaller, "cheap" disk drives – used together in novel ways – which you could pair with more expensive computer systems. They reckoned that this disk group could provide greater efficiency and faster I/O performance than their mainframe disk storage counterparts.

- The grouping of several small disk drives that could successfully survive a failure of any one disk drive. They said this arrangement would prove more reliable than mainframe disk storage.

The paper, and its early RAID concepts, revolutionized the storage industry. Throughout the 90's storage vendors quickly embraced this technology. Today, every storage array vendor uses some form of RAID technology to protect against disk drive failures.

> **Bits & Bytes:** Although Gibson and his co-authors effectively defined the five initial RAID levels, they neither patented their definitions nor trademarked the term RAID. In Gibson's view, those decisions helped fuel the eventual growth and pervasiveness of RAID. "If we had patented the name and taxonomy for, say, RAID level 5, then the majority of companies would not have used it," Gibson said. "The benefits that it has provided as an organizing principle would simply not have happened."[11]

RAID: A Closer Look

The Berkeley paper went on to describe five different RAID methods (RAID 1 through RAID 5) many of which are still in use today.

We're not going to give a detailed RAID primer here. There are plenty of those around online. Table 2-1 (on the next page), however, summarizes the key differences between popular RAID levels.

Table 2-1. Key RAID Techniques.

RAID Technique (RAID Example)	Description
No Parity (RAID 0)	Although not described in the original Berkeley paper, RAID 0 became a popular way to increase I/O performance by striping (or logically distributing) data across several disk drives. Note that RAID 0 offered no protection against failed disk drives.
Mirroring (RAID 1)	With RAID 1, data is "mirrored" onto a second set of disks without using parity. Although able to survive multiple drive failures, RAID 1's disk mirroring exacts a high capacity penalty.
Fixed Parity (RAID 3 / RAID 4)	RAID 3 and RAID 4 both use parity calculations (sometimes known as checksum) to perform error-checking. These RAID levels use algorithms allowing the recovery of missing data from failed drives. They reconstruct the data with data and parity from the remaining (functional) drives. With fixed parity, the parity information is stored on dedicated disk drives in the RAID set.
Striped Parity (RAID 5)	Similar to Fixed Parity, RAID 5 parity is "striped" (or logically distributed) across all disks in the RAID set in an attempt to boost RAID read/write performance.
Multiple Parity (RAID 6)	Newer RAID levels (like RAID 6) offer higher levels of protection. They do this by using multiple iterations of fixed or striped parity on a group of drives, which allows for multiple drive failures without data loss.

Today: Emerging RAID Efficiencies

In choosing the appropriate RAID level, a storage vendor (and storage user) creates a balance between three factors:

- Read/write performance impact of RAID implementations
- Greater (or lesser) disk failure protection and array reliability
- The capacity overhead needed to support a specific RAID implementation

Since the Berkeley paper, many storage vendors have added their own flavors of RAID in an effort to improve their storage array's performance, disk failure protection and/or affordability. Examples of this include RAID 10 (striping + mirroring), and double (or triple) parity RAID.

Not all have managed to strike the most efficient balance between these three areas. In the next few pages, I'll offer NetApp as a comparative model that's evolved to demonstrate balanced, efficient RAID usage in a modern-day storage array.

Modeling Efficient RAID Performance, Utilization and Protection

NetApp made an early decision to implement RAID 4—followed by its implementation of multiple-parity RAID—both of which proved key to the company's RAID efficiency model.

We'll look at each of these designs below.

Gaining Efficiency from an Unlikely Source: RAID 4

At the time NetApp first chose to support RAID 4 in 1992 with its original product release, the company broke from tradition. The favored RAID levels of the time were RAID 0 (no parity but very fast), RAID 1 (mirroring) and RAID 5 (striped parity).

Why did NetApp take this route? Most vendors discarded RAID 4 due to a perceived significant write performance penalty. NetApp's WAFL (Write Anywhere File Layout) core system technology, however, offered a different performance profile that made RAID 4 the better choice.

The difference related to WAFL's efficient method of write allocation. A 2007 NetApp Tech OnTap article,[12] "The Core NetApp DNA," describes this early NetApp efficiency with RAID 4 in more technical detail.

"WAFL is the Write Anywhere File Layout, an approach to writing data to disk locations that minimizes the conventional parity RAID write penalty . . . This approach, in turn, allows multiple writes to be "gathered" and scheduled to the same RAID stripe—eliminating the traditional read-modify-write penalty prevalent in parity-based RAID schemes.

In the case of WAFL, this stripe-at-a-time write approach makes RAID 4 a viable (and even preferred) parity scheme. At the time of its design, the common wisdom was that RAID 4 (which uses a dedicated parity drive) presented a bottleneck for write operations because writes that would otherwise be spread across the data drives would all have to update the single parity drive in the RAID group. WAFL and full-stripe writes, however, eliminate the potential bottleneck and, in fact, provide a highly optimized write path.

This stripe-at-a-time approach to writes also required that the system provide a means of reliably buffering write requests before they are written (en masse) to disk. Nonvolatile RAM allows the system to reliably log writes and quickly acknowledge those writes back to clients."

This combination of RAID 4 with parity stripes and NVRAM provided a unique proposition: The I/O performance of RAID 0 and the disk drive failure protection of RAID 5.

RAID Efficiency With 'Cheap-and-Big' SATA Drives

When more affordable, large capacity Serial ATA (SATA) drives first appeared in the market, they exhibited significantly higher failure rates than the norm. For this reason, they were not typically recommended for enterprise production applications. They were relegated, instead, to the bottom tiers of storage.

Data center managers still appreciated SATA's affordable price/capacity profile, however. Many storage vendors responded to the continued SATA interest by deploying SATA-based arrays with traditional RAID 5 support. They reasoned this would allow the array to remain in operation even when faced with the failure of a single disk in the RAID group.

Users, however, were reluctant to embrace this idea due to a few associated risks:

- Data rebuild times on larger SATA drives would take a very long time (many hours or, even, days).
- Data loss would result if a second disk failure occurred in the same RAID group during the time the first disk's rebuild process was still underway.

Vendors struggled with this and eventually came up with the idea of "dual-parity" RAID. The idea being that multiple iterations of parity would protect against an unlikely (but not impossible) multiple-drive failure event. NetApp again took a slightly different approach with the company's RAID-DP breakthrough, first described in a 2004 paper, *"Row-Diagonal Parity for Double Disk Failure Correction."*[13]

RAID-DP (the "DP" stands for Double Parity) builds on the company's prior RAID 4 functionality. It uses a second, diagonal parity method to ensure the RAID array will survive not just one, but two concurrent disk drive failures in the same RAID group.

Most multiple parity RAID implementations suffer a significant degradation in disk write performance. Those did not bear out with NetApp, WAFL and RAID-DP. The difference between "traditional" RAID implementations and NetApp's RAID-DP is described, as follows:

> "[Traditional] RAID-6 adds an additional parity block and provides approximately double the data protection over RAID-5, but at a cost of even lower write performance . . .
>
> Unlike traditional RAID-6, RAID-DP utilizes diagonal parity using two dedicated parity disks in the RAID group. RAID-DP is also similar to other RAID-6 implementations in terms of the reliability metrics and its ability to survive the loss of any two disks; however, a third disk failure will result in data loss.
>
> Whereas current RAID-6 implementations incur an I/O performance penalty as a result of introducing an additional parity block, RAID-DP is optimized in terms of reducing [write] I/Os due to the way the NetApp controller handles parity write operations. Unlike other storage controllers that write changes to the original location, the NetApp controller always writes data to new blocks, thus making random writes appear to be written sequentially."

RAID continues to be the primary method of enterprise disk drive and SSD protection with the latest iteration being triple-parity RAID, which affords an additional layer of insurance in that it can survive the concurrent failure of three devices with a RAID set.

The Future: Erasure Coding and Data Placement

Modern-day RAID's data recovery properties allow the storage controller to not just detect drive failure, but automatically rebuild the data while the storage system continues to remain up and running.

Although storage systems have learned to heal themselves when disk drives fail, an evolution is taking place in two specific areas with techniques that arguably do a better job of protecting from hardware failures:

- **Erasure Coding** is an advanced form of RAID in which data is broken into fragments, encoded, and stored across multiple storage devices in different locations. If any fragments become lost or corrupted, they can be recreated using the encoded data stored with the remaining fragments. The main advantage of Erasure Coding is that devices do not need to be physically "grouped" as is the case with traditional RAID, rather, fragments can exist anywhere as long as they are accessible by the storage controller, making this an attractive alternative in very large and broadly dispersed data sets. The drawback of Erasure Coding is that it can be more CPU-intensive than RAID reconstructions, which can translate into increased latencies as fragments are recovered.

- **Data Placement** refers to a new method of data protection that doesn't offer any data reconstruction all – instead these systems carefully make data copies and spread them across a network of storage nodes, with each node being an independent entity from all other nodes. The number of copies can usually be defined by the user – more copies offer greater protection but also consume more storage. If a storage controller fails to read the expected data from a damaged or missing node, it simply goes to an alternate node to retrieve to data.

Data Placement - A Workaround for Drive Rebuilds?

A pioneer in the use of data placement philosophy is Amazon's Dynamo infrastructure. With over one trillion data objects now stored in its data centers, Amazon has quickly become one of the largest storage consumers in the world.[14] Storing that many objects requires tens of thousands of disk drives. For Amazon, that means disk drive failure is not just a potential occurrence. It's a certainty. To deal with this reality, Amazon simply allows disk drives to fail without any RAID protection at all. Instead, the company uses a system it calls "eventual consistency," described in a paper by Amazon Web Services CTO Werner Vogels and others.[15]

The technical details in Vogels' paper are quite complex, but the way Dynamo works can be explained simply. Dynamo is a distributed storage system. It uses a relational database that contains information about all stored data objects. All objects are, thus, stored and looked up via a unique key. Central to Dynamo's protection against failed disk drives is its ability to create many copies of each object and share the objects amongst many storage nodes, located on physically dispersed disk drives.

As data is written by Dynamo, one node updates object A, and propagates the changes to all other nodes which store copies of object A. This is performed asynchronously, which is why the system is called "eventually consistent."

While technically complex, Dynamo is still conceptually simple. It is inspired by the way things work in nature—based on self-organization and emergence. For instance:

- Each node is identical to other nodes

- The nodes can come in and out of existence

- Data is automatically balanced around a ring of nodes

All of this makes Dynamo able to operate autonomously with commodity hardware that is expected to fail.

The Future of Protection: What's in Store?

As we look back and, then, toward the future regarding storage hardware failures and the ways around them, it's easy to make a few conclusions.

Most of these stem from the belief that the storage array's efforts to protect against failure will need to start occurring *long before* the hardware actually registers failure. The body of evolution in this area will occur more in terms of early diagnosis and prevention than it will be in the area of post-mortem fixes.

With that in mind, here are a few specific thoughts on where we are headed:

- **RAID can only go so far.** Modern-day RAID data protection is an extremely useful and necessary recovery measure. Yet, it is believed by many that continued disk drive (and SSD) capacity growth will soon outpace RAID's ability to keep up.

  Many storage vendors are now exploring triple-parity RAID protection (that protects against the concurrent failure of three disks in the same RAID group) but, how far can this go? We will likely see 50TB drives in the next 5-10 years.

  In that case, how many RAID parity blocks are enough? Some people have a hard time seeing the industry moving RAID into areas like quadruple or quintuple parity RAID protection. Instead, storage array vendors must develop a new paradigm surrounding protection against device failures.

- **An ounce of prevention is worth a pound of cure.** Much as early "well-care" visits to the doctor can identify (and potentially avert) initial warning signs of a more serious problem, early diagnosis of potential hardware health issues and their prescription to avert a future event should lead to significant reductions in failures themselves.

  It's a paradigm shift from the post-mortem autopsies typically performed by RAID technology and more toward a model of preventative medicine. Look for advances in the area of pre-failure detection and proactive corrective measures.

- **Hardware in "sick" mode.** When you aren't feeling well, what do you do? Cancel meetings, limit exposure to others, curtail activities and, in general, just rest until you feel better. This is the body's way of saying, "Hey, I need some time to heal."

Why shouldn't storage hardware have the same intelligence? Slow down the moving parts, signal to the storage controller that something isn't quite right, let the storage controller make a house call and prescribe a corrective action plan. Such a plan might include something as simple as a power-on reset, or something as drastic as copying data to another node and permanently powering down the offending component.

Endnotes Referenced in Chapter 2

10 http://www.eecs.berkeley.edu/Pubs/TechRpts/1987/5853.html.
11 http://www.internetnews.com/storage/article.php/3514651.
12 http://partners.netapp.com/go/techontap/matl/NetApp_DNA.html.
13 http://www.usenix.org/events/fast04/tech/corbett/corbett.pdf.
14 http://www.zdnet.com/blog/btl/amazon-s3-hits-one-trillion-objects/79793
15 http://www.allthingsdistributed.com/files/amazon-dynamo-sosp2007.pdf.

***

Chapter Three: Virus? What Virus?

Your computer has been encrypted

The hard disks of your computer have been encrypted with an military grade encryption algorithm. It's impossible to recover your data without an special key. This page will help you with the purchase of this key and the complete decryption of your computer.

⏱ The price will be doubled in:

6 days 13 hours 43 minutes 10 seconds

☑ Start the decryption process

Ransomware is the latest in a long string of attempts to compromise your data. Once this malware installs covertly on a victim's computer, a cryptovirus attack is made on personal files, and a ransom payment is demanded in order to decrypt the files.

Ransomware attacks are typically carried out using a Trojan that has a payload disguised as a legitimate file. Variants may also encrypt the computer's Master File Table (MFT) or the entire hard drive. This denial-of-access attack has affected a surprising number of enterprise servers, including those maintained by government and law enforcement officials.[16]

* * *

Extending Data Protection Beyond Disk Drives

In the last chapter, we discussed protection against failed hardware. Yet, even if we were to eventually evolve technology to the point that hardware never failed, you still couldn't sleep easy. Even with a perfectly tuned storage system, data loss or corruption can still occur, as illustrated by the ransomware example on this chapter's title page.

This chapter presents the second half of protection's evolution. Here, we focus on emerging technologies and practices that protect the *whole* storage system, including the data itself.

Common Causes of Data Loss and Corruption

Outside of disk drive failure, just how prevalent is data loss or corruption? Figure 3-1 offers one glimpse of its potential causes. According to SunGard Availability Services, data corruption was its fastest growing cause of business disruption in the U.K., falling just behind hardware and power issues.[17]

Figure 3-1. Leading Causes of Data Loss.[18]

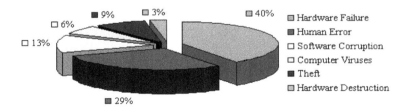

As we continue our discussion on protection against data loss and corruption, here are some potential causes to consider:

- **Accidental data deletion.** Like many causes, this one falls into the larger category of "human error."
- **Lost or misplaced writes.** These types of errors can occur when a disk drive indicates a block of data has been written to disk when, in fact: A) It hasn't been written to disk at all, or B) its been written to the wrong place on disk. A number of other "disk subtleties" are also noted in a Berkeley paper[19] as the source of potential data errors.
- **A malicious attack or computer virus.** This includes malicious software that runs amok or a wider attack impacting a region and all the companies, individuals and systems within it.
- **Accidental data corruption.** Applications, like the humans that create them, are not perfect and have been known to corrupt their own data due to insidious software bugs.
- **Acts of Terrorism.** Terrorist attacks can paralyze entire cities. Even if people and buildings are fortunate enough to survive, you may lose access to your data for an extended period of time due to power losses and travel restrictions.
- **An Act of God.** Natural disasters–things like floods, hurricanes, earthquakes and tornadoes--can wreak havoc on an organization's data. These events, however rare, can lead to a site-wide disaster that includes destruction of equipment and the data contained on impacted systems.

Dealing with Data Loss

The data storage industry adopted two specific approaches in response to the threat of data loss or corruption: Data replication and data backup.

Each is discussed briefly in Table 3-1.

Table 3-1. Approaches to Data Loss or Corruption.

Approach	Description
Data replication	Data replication can be thought of as 'mirroring' critical data to an alternate location. Replication is typically performed in anticipation of a potential, catastrophic event that could come between you and your data. Nearly all enterprises today have some sort of disaster recovery plan calling for a second data set to be stored at an alternate location in case of an emergency. Volumes of information have been written on disaster recovery planning, so we won't attempt to cover this topic here. Here is a list a few resources for further research: DRI, The Institute for Continuity Management Disaster Recovery Journal International Disaster Recovery Association Business Continuity Management Institute
Data backup	As the name implies, data backup refers to the practice of preserving backup copies of data for somewhat mundane reasons. This could include wanting to restore data that may have been accidentally deleted. It could also include the need to refer back to an earlier data version or copy. In either case, backups provide an easy mechanism to accomplish this. Data backup is a topic we will cover in some detail in this chapter.

The Past: The Tale of the Tape

In the early days of mainframes and minicomputers, magnetic tape was the "king" of storage. Back then, tape wasn't thought of so much as a backup medium. Rather, it was where you stored your data when it wasn't being processed on disk. There just wasn't enough room on disk to store infrequently used data.

As disk systems got larger and computers became more powerful, however, tape fell into the role of preserving, protecting and restoring (when needed) critical data sets. Tape provided something indispensable over disk systems of the time: A pristine copy of your data that could be stored in an alternate (and presumably safer) location.

Tape: Then and Now

As mentioned in Chapter 1, IBM's RAMAC 305 computer ushered in the new magnetic disk era with the introduction of its IBM 350 storage unit in 1956. However, fully 5 years earlier in 1951, Eckert-Mauchly Computer Corporation's UNIVAC 1[20] introduced the world's first magnetic digital tape drive.

The UNIVAC's UNISERVO tape drive used 1200-foot-long, reel-based tape. It was able to record data on eight separate channels at a rate of 7200 characters per second and a density of 128 bits per inch.[21] (Figure 3-2 shows a bank of UNISERVO tape drives associated with the UNIVAC 1's first customer: The U.S. Census Bureau.)

Figure 3-2. UNIVSERVO: The First Digital Tape Drive.[22]

Before long, institutions and government entities needing to protect their growing stores of data had to devote whole rooms to the storage of these types of tapes. Figure 3-3 shows just a glimpse of the amount of tape storage needed in those days.

Figure 3-3. Early Reel-Based Tape Storage, Columbia University.[23]

Today's Backup Tapes

Since the days of reel-based tape, backup tapes have gone through numerous iterations and formats, including a move to compact cartridges of various shapes and sizes.

Throughout the 80s and 90s, "tape format wars" ensued amongst tape drive vendors fighting for market share. Sample formats from this era included:

- Quarter-Inch Cartridge (QIC)
- 4mm or 8mm Tape
- Digital Linear Tape (DLT)
- Advanced Intelligent Tape (AIT)
- Linear Tape Open (LTO)

Today, the war has ended and LTO has become the reigning tape format for the majority of users. Suppliers of the current generation LTO-7 tape drive include HP, IBM, Quantum and Tandberg Data.

Figure 3-4. LTO Tape Drive

The Trouble with Tape

Through much of the early days of data storage, data stored on magnetic tape was considered much simpler and more reliable than its disk-based counterparts. Tape, however, has a less than stellar reputation today. The reasons for this are explained below.

Nightly backup windows exceeded. Exponential data growth has led to longer and longer nightly tape backup windows. Fueling this problem, the modern linear tape format requires a steady stream of data pumped to it from application servers. Any interruption in this data feed results in the dreaded "shoe-shining" effect. Because of this, backup administrators have often had to compromise by:

- Only backing up the most critical data.
- Stopping nightly backups before they completed.
- Running backups into the next day's business hours, potentially impacting operation of production systems.

Tape media management headaches. As a removable medium, tape media requires prudence once it is ejected from its parent device and stored outside the data center. Tape backups are often stored and must be retrieved in 'sets'. The failure to produce a single tape can render an entire backup set unusable. Similarly, the failure of a single tape during a restore operation can result in dire consequences.

Mechanical issues. Tape drives and tape libraries have by far the greatest number of precisely moving mechanical parts of any device in the data center. As a tape cartridge is loaded, positioned, and unloaded during a backup job, it results in a symphony of coordinated movements of robotics, gripper arms, load and eject mechanisms, capstans, pinch rollers, and leader threading assemblies. While vendors have improved the precision of these movements, the possibility of mechanical failure remains troublesome for many tape users today.

For many of these reasons, the storage industry has sought a better, more efficient alternative to nightly tape-based data backups. However, it wouldn't be until the start of the twenty-first century that the industry could fully embrace a new paradigm: D2D (disk-to-disk backup).

Recent History: Early Tape Backup Automation

Initially, tape backups were as unintelligent as the devices performing the backup tasks. A few rudimentary system commands (notably UNIX commands *tar*, *dd*, *cpio*, *dump/restore* – and later *ntbackup* from Microsoft) were either run manually or scripted to run late at night or on weekends. These were run with the hope that they'd complete successfully in the early hours of the morning.

This paradigm changed in 1988, however, when a company with roots in Sun Microsystems was formed. The company was Legato and was responsible for introducing a novel software product called Networker. (Legato has since been acquired by EMC.)

At the beginning, Networker offered a few welcome additions to the world of tape backup. With Networker:

- Backups could be scheduled through a convenient graphical user interface (scripts not required).
- Failed backup jobs could be rescheduled automatically.
- Backup summary reports were produced to verify successful backups.
- A catalog of all backup files could be created, allowing users to query for a particular file they wanted to recover.

Soon, other backup software vendors began to appear. These vendors began to experiment with methods to overcome the inherent shortcomings of tape-based data protection. A few efforts involved smarter use of tape.

Still others involved early use of disk as the intermediary. Table 3-2 describes a few of these concepts. Many of these are still used today, including the use of disk as the primary backup device.

Table 3-2. Data Backup Innovations.

Tape-Based Innovations:	
Interleaving	This practice improved tape backup speeds by allowing backups to be written to multiple tapes concurrently. By writing to several tapes in parallel, individual backup jobs could be completed faster. Interleaving, however, required a significant amount of processing power on the part of the application server. This practice also increased the risk of a failed restore, since one bad tape could render an entire backup unreadable.
Synthetic Backup	Recognizing the time it took to perform frequent full backups to tape, and the complexity of interleaving, vendors like Tivoli (later acquired by IBM) pioneered the concept of performing an "incremental forever" backup policy.[24] This technique required just a single full backup and used an intermediate database to track and map the location of the continuous incremental backups performed to tape thereafter.
Reclamation	Also pioneered by Tivoli Storage Manager (TSM), the tape reclamation process solved a problem created by Synthetic tape backups. As backups expired they would create data "holes" in existing backup tapes. By performing a periodic reclamation operation, the contents of partially filled backup tapes could be consolidated onto fewer tapes. The reclamation process, however, proved cumbersome as data sizes grew, with backup tapes becoming more difficult to either track or reclaim.

Disk-Based Innovations:	
Disk Staging	By the late '80s, IBM had already begun to describe the concept of early disk staging. In this case, IBM documentation described data stored on optical media that could be moved by a staging manager to magnetic disk drives. These drives would then serve as a faster, more accessible "online archive" which could be used to send the data to tape without affecting production workloads. Early disk staging to tape evolved from backup software vendors like Veritas (now Symantec), Legato, and Computer Associates.
D2D2T	Intermediate disk staging soon became known as D2D2T (disk-to-disk-to-tape). Benefits of D2D2T included faster backups and faster restores, due in large part to disk's faster random access and better striping functionality. Many D2D2T solutions also allowed faster data streaming to tape, which avoided the typical tape "shoe-shining" process. Also, because at least one night's backup was stored on disk, restoration of data could be performed from disk much more quickly than from tape.
D2D	As disk drive capacities increased and new features (like data compression and deduplication) were introduced, users were able to first consider the possibility of disk-to-disk (D2D) backup without tape. The concept of tapeless backup, while intriguing, is most likely not sustainable for a number of reasons to be covered later in this chapter.

The Modern Age: Emerging D2D Efficiencies

As identified in the prior table, disk-based backup solutions began to gain significant popularity due to increased storage system intelligence beginning around 2001. Using disk, users could take advantage of the emerging high capacity, lower cost ATA disk drives available on the market. ATA–paired with disk-based efficiencies such as data compression and deduplication– was an obvious marriage.

D2D solutions and their underlying architectures continue to be popular today. Using today's efficiencies, D2D backup costs are on par with traditional tape backups. The added convenience of reliable, near-instantaneous data recovery has brought joy to the hearts of storage administrators.

For data backups, tape is out; and disk is in. But after 60 years, tape (like disk) will not completely disappear. Disk does not have the permanence or the areal storage density of tape. No study suggests that a disk drive can be placed on the shelf for years and be expected to spin up and recover data. This has been a proven value of tape for decades, and will continue as such as the method for longer term archival.

Does The Future of Data Protection Lie in The Cloud?

So, beyond D2D, what does the future hold for protection against lost or corrupt data? Having spent several decades working within this segment of the industry, I am here to say that this market is in the midst of dramatic change.

Data backups are big business. By my count, there are well over 50 companies today providing products that power enterprise IT backups. These products fall into four general categories:

- Tape-based backup appliances
- D2D backup appliances
- Enterprise backup software
- Enterprise backup to the cloud

Interestingly, the "backup to the cloud" group is the largest and fastest growing of these categories. Most of the products (and companies) in this category did not even exist when my book *Evolution of the Storage Brain* was released in 2010. Why is this? Is the cloud a perfect destination for your backups?

To answer that question, let's look first at the traditional model of backup. This is where software-controlled dedicated servers would sit on-premise and perform data backups to either an onsite or offsite location. This traditional model, although with us for decades, developed a reputation of being very complex to administer and very expensive to maintain. If fact, you may have known someone that held the title "backup administrator" in IT, and if so, you might agree that this person was usually not a very friendly fellow. (If you were that person, please accept my condolences).

Cloud backups, in contrast, are changing this traditional backup model. As cloud computing and cloud storage become more prominent, applications, users, and data are becoming distributed. Because of this, cloud backups are compelling. They don't require a large, up-front investment in equipment, are fairly easy to administer, and remove one more task from often overburdened IT administrators.

Like so many other applications that have sprouted from the public cloud, individual users first used the cloud to perform their own personal backups. This eventually worked its way up to small and medium-sized businesses.   Now it seems that cloud backups are destined for enterprise users as well.

Bandwidth: Cloud's Final Frontier for the Enterprise

The limiting factor today for enterprise cloud backup is bandwidth, or specifically, the lack of bandwidth. By IT standards, data travels relatively slowly to and from the clouds. Initial baseline backups can take days or weeks to accomplish over a standard Internet connection.

A once-thought-fast T1 connection moves data at 1.544 megabits per second, meaning that the transfer of 1TB of data takes approximately 59 days. This may be fine for single users or even small organizations, but it's woefully slow for enterprise IT.

Because of these WAN speeds, cloud-based backups are often "seeded" by physically shipping disk drives of even entire storage arrays in order to provide a baseline copy of data at the cloud provider's site (Amazon's Snowball[25] service being one example of this). Once the baseline backup data is seeded, small backups are sent each night containing just the data that changed since the prior night's backup in order to be completed quickly. Again, okay for small to medium companies, but not for large organizations.

Luckily, faster network connections are available. T3 connections and a set of OC (optical carrier) standards have become increasingly affordable and suitable for larger, online cloud-based backup sets.

Table 3-3 shows how such faster connections now offer
more opportunity for cloud backup.

Table 3-3. Carriers and Their Corresponding Transfer Speeds and Time.

Carrier Type	Speed	Equivalent	Time to Transfer 1TB
T1	1.544 megabits/sec.	N/A	59 Days
T3	43.232 megabits/sec.	28 T1 lines	2 Days
OC3	155 megabits/sec.	84 T1 lines	14 Hours
OC12	622 megabits/sec.	4 OC3 lines	4 Hours
OC48	2.5 gigabits/sec.	4 OC12 lines	1 Hour
OC192	9.6 gigabits/sec.	4 OC48 lines	15 Minutes

Note that the "Time to Transfer" column is based on
the rated speed of each connection type. While actual
speeds may be slower due to distance latencies, etc., this
chart serves to illustrate the dramatic WAN speed
increases now available that make large cloud backups
feasible.

> **Tape vs. Cloud in the Real World:** The Spiceworks
> community offers an interesting exchange[26] in this area. Here,
> users try to understand the real-world bandwidth issues, costs
> and concerns that pertain to tape versus cloud as the
> mechanism to back up over 5TB of data.

Cloud backups are working their way up the data
ladder. There seems to be little doubt that more and more
organizations will soon be handing backup duties over to
their chosen cloud provider.

In future, IT administrators may be able to sleep a
little easier knowing their data is protected from mischief
and now safely tucked away in the cloud!

Endnotes Referenced in Chapter 3

16 http://www.heraldbulletin.com/news/local_news/ransomware-attack-hits-county-government/article_55d6cf6e-a39b-11e6-841e-dbc3d34efcf2.html
17 http://www.continuitycentral.com/news04599.html.
18 http://gbr.pepperdine.edu/033/dataloss.html.
19 http://www.cs.berkeley.edu/~krioukov/parityLost.pdf.
20 http://en.wikipedia.org/wiki/UNIVAC_I.
21 http://en.wikipedia.org/wiki/UNISERVO.
22 Image Source: Wikipedia. Photo caption reads: "Remington Rand employees, Harold E. Sweeney (left) and J. Presper Eckert (center) demonstrate the U.S. Census Bureau's UNIVAC for CBS reporter Walter Cronkite (right)."
23 http://www.columbia.edu/acis/history/1965.html.
24 http://www-01.ibm.com/support/docview.wss?crawler=1&uid=swg27002265.
25 http://docs.aws.amazon.com/snowball/latest/ug/whatissnowball.html
26 http://community.spiceworks.com/topic/125042-backup-5-tb-of-data-cloud-based-or-tape-and-why

***

Chapter Four: Journey To The Center Of The Storage Brain

The above image depicts an early storage controller manufactured by Dilog, circa 1979. Dilog's DQ132 was a Q-Bus controller that was primarily OEMed to Digital Equipment Corporation for use in its VAX and PDP computers.[27] During the era of "dumb" storage, this board represented the entire storage brain and was responsible for sending and receiving all information to and from the four tape drives that were directly cabled.

* * *

Controllers: At the "Heart" of the Matter

We began our discussion of the history of data storage with the disk drive, followed by discussions of evolving protection of both disk drives and data. In this chapter, we'll begin to uncover data storage's basic building blocks, starting with the CPU itself.

This is the central core of any storage system, the heart of the matter, the "engine" without which today's modern-day storage systems would cease to function. For the purpose of this book, you might even think of it as the overall storage brain.

What we're talking about is the evolution of the modern-day *storage array controller* (*storage controller* for short), which drives today's storage system intelligence.

Looking under the hood of a modern-day storage controller, you see an evolving set of microprocessors. These operate at breakneck speeds and are kept busy receiving and sending core instructions throughout the storage system's neural network.

(While memory is another core piece of today's storage controller, it is such an important component that we've opted to describe it fully in the next chapter.)

For this chapter, we'll look more specifically at the role of early disk controllers, microprocessors, and modern-day storage controllers. We'll also explore the trends behind ever more powerful storage brains and what they'll mean to the data storage industry in the future.

The Past: Refrigerators and Cards

As noted in Chapter 1, early disk drives in the mainframe era were typically managed by what amounted to a refrigerator-sized disk channel controller.

This bulky controller appears in Figure 4-1[28] shows a seated mainframe operator with a bank of IBM disk drives (circa 1975) behind him. The figure also shows a channel controller to the right side of the bank of drives.

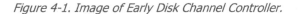
Figure 4-1. Image of Early Disk Channel Controller.

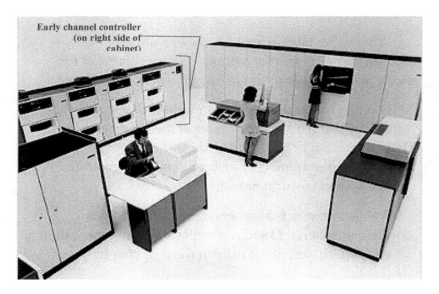

This controller was responsible for processing commands and data transfers between the mainframe and one or more disks typically daisy-chained together in a channel, via bus-and-tag cabling (if you've been paying attention, this should all sound familiar!)

> **The Cray and Early Disk Controllers:** Early Cray Research
> documentation from the 1970s describes its 819 Disk
> Controller as being "packaged in a Freon-controlled cabinet."[29]
> The controller was required to be placed close to the Cray-1
> supercomputer mainframe. It allowed for 1-4 Control Data
> 819 disk storage units to be attached to it.

As the era of minicomputers emerged in the early
'70s, disk drives and disk controllers began to shrink –
thanks in part to that nifty invention – the integrated
circuit (IC). CDC's new SMD disk drive interface
utilizing ICs prompted a move away from refrigerator-
sized disk controllers.

With the growing popularity of SMD disk drives, disk
controllers became available which could be inserted as a
board into the minicomputer's CPU card cage.

SMD disk controller cards were manufactured by a
number of companies, notably Dilog, Ciprico and
Xylogics (the Xylogics 431 controller is shown in Figure 4-
2). These controllers were used by minicomputers as well
as early UNIX workstations of the '80s. They were valued
for their relatively low-cost in comparison to their more
expensive mainframe counterparts.

Figure 4-2. The Xylogics 431 Disk Controller Could Control Four SMD Disk Drives.[30]

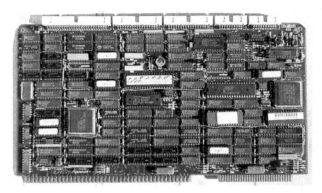

Still relatively simple in operation, these early disk controller cards had, nonetheless, begun to take the first few steps toward evolving intelligence. Integrated circuit board designs allowed storage controllers to begin to function independently. This was the start of the modern storage brain: A logical entity with its own processing power now responsible for carrying out instructions to and from disk. Such evolution was distinctly different from earlier controllers that relied predominantly on the processing capabilities of the mainframe.

Microprocessors and Moore's Famous Law

The move from computer-based to board-based disk controller intelligence (like that of the Xylogics card) was made possible by another set of early events that would change not just disk storage. They would also spawn the age of personal computers.

Table 4-1. Technological Events Influencing Future Storage Controllers.

Year	Event
1961	**Commercial release of the first integrated circuit.** Based on research breakthroughs pioneered separately by Jack Kilby (then of Texas Instruments) and Robert Noyce (then of Fairchild Computer Corporation), the first commercial integrated circuit appeared from Fairchild in 1961. Unlike prior, complex circuit boards, the IC was able to combine more transistors, resistors, a capacitor and the underlying wiring all on a single chip. Subsequent computers would use this chip instead of all the discrete components they'd needed to incorporate before.[31]
1965	**Moore's Law came into existence.** Another Fairchild colleague of Noyce's at the time, Gordon C. Moore, produced a paper in the mid-60s postulating that the number of components on a circuit board could conceivably double in size every year for the next 10 years. Now widely known as Moore's law, Moore updated his early prognosis in 1975 to the expectation that processing power would double every 24 months. Moore's law would prove consistently true for the next 20 years, as innovation in chip design continued to double processing power – up to well into the 2000s.
1968	**Intel Corporation was founded.** The introduction of the IC was followed in 1968 by the founding of Intel Corporation (by Noyce and Gordon Moore). Intel would ultimately become the world's largest maker of semiconductor chips.
1971	**Commercial release of the Intel 4004, the first single-chip microprocessor.** To aid an early Japanese client (Busicom), Intel's 4004 chip placed the following functions on the same chip for the first time: The central processing unit (CPU), memory and input/output controls. This would be the precursor for Intel's successful x86 chips that drove the adoption of early IBM PCs of the '80s. Without the emergence and evolution of CPUs on their own microprocessor "chip," early storage controllers might well have remained primitive.

> **The Microprocessor and a Hen House?** Given the prevalence of today's microprocessor, it's hard to imagine its somewhat odd beginnings. In an interview, Gordon Moore recalled an early use of the microprocessor: Aiding the automation of hen houses. Moore said that early customer use of the microprocessor was so odd it even prompted one Intel board member to ask him if the company was ever going to get a customer he'd heard of before.[32]

The Age of RAID Controllers

The 1980s saw Intel, AMD and other chip manufacturers race to release ever-faster microprocessors. The rising tide of fast chip technology carried with it growing innovation in a variety of computer industries. This proved especially true in the storage industry as well.

The introduction of RAID storage (as discussed in Chapter 2 and in the epic '80s Berkeley paper) was tied to the increase in server processing capabilities. It was also tied to the need to cost-effectively "keep up" with the inherent data I/O and reliability demands of applications running on these faster systems.

However, RAID also gave birth to an important evolution of storage intelligence: The RAID controller. RAID controllers combined the basic functionality of disk controllers with the ability to group drives together for added performance and reliability. During this period, Emulex and Adaptec emerged as the dominant suppliers of RAID controllers.

RAID controllers took advantage of the newly found processing power of the day, using this power to add important storage functionality. As the name implied, RAID controllers were responsible for implementing

RAID operations, such as creating and managing RAID groups[33] and rebuilding data from failed disks.

Storage controllers were becoming more sophisticated; and being given more responsibility. Functionality within early RAID controllers included:

- Communication between the underlying disks (referred to as the back-end interface) and the attached host computer (referred to as the front-end interface).

  This could be thought of as an internal network which evolved within the overall storage brain. Among other things, this network allowed the RAID controller to communicate with its underlying disk drives independently. (We'll describe more about the evolution of the storage brain's internal and external networks in a later chapter on the storage nervous system.)

- Protection against disk failure through the creation of one or more RAID groups (see Chapter 2 for more on RAID and related disk protection functions)

- Dual-controller systems, which could be used for added performance, availability and automated failover. These systems allowed one RAID controller to "take over" in the event of failure of the other controller. This is equivalent to two sides of the human brain operating in tandem, with either an Active/Active or Active/Passive configuration that allows recovery and continued storage operation without exposure of any issues to the outside world.

During this era, anyone with a screwdriver and a little patience could build themselves a nice little RAID storage system using readily available off-the-shelf parts – and sell them to storage-hungry users for a tidy profit.

Storage was getting cheaper and more reliable. This was a good thing because a data explosion was about to occur. As we approached the '90s, data became more critical and grew faster than anyone could have imagined. The idea of the intelligent *storage array controller* was beginning to take hold, and a new industry was about to emerge.

The Modern Age: Storage Array Controllers

Introduced in 1990, the EMC Symmetrix contained arguably the world's first integrated storage array controller. With a whopping 23GB of online storage, EMC advertised the Symmetrix as an "integrated cached storage array." First targeted as a replacement for IBM mainframe 3390 disk storage systems (with bus-and-tag cabling), EMC later developed a "platform independent" version of the Symmetrix, supporting all popular interfaces.[34]

> **Who Had the First Array Controller?** Some may argue that the Auspex Systems NS 5000, introduced in 1987, lays claim as the world's first storage array controller. While Auspex did introduce the world's first dedicated, networked storage appliance, a peek inside the original Auspex design revealed a Sun SPARC workstation operating inside as its 'brain.' This disqualifies Auspex from being a truly integrated storage array.

As other companies followed suit with EMC, the storage array quickly became a purpose-built standalone computer – containing an array of disk drives, a specialized CPU, memory, power supplies, operating system and management software.

Modern-day networked storage was born.

The storage industry became very volatile during the '90s. Old-school storage suppliers (such as once-favored companies like Pyramid Technologies and Systems Industries) faded away while innovative companies like EMC and NetApp capitalized on increased storage intelligence. They subsequently grew at a record pace.

Storage companies were coming and going at such a dizzying pace it was hard to keep up with all the changes.

For example, Auspex was an early favorite during this era with its concept of network-attached storage, but quickly disappeared when it failed to recognize that customers did not want or need sophisticated Symmetrix-like features for network-attached storage.

Witness Auspex CEO Larry Boucher's prophetic comments in an interview from this period:[35]

> **The Herring:** We talked about your big competitors. Are there any private companies that you see coming downstream that are producing interesting technologies that might be competitive with Auspex?
>
> **Boucher:** The only private company that I'm aware of is NAC -- Network Appliance Corporation. NAC is comprised of people who were very early employees at Auspex that left to build their own company. NAC is building a PC-based product, and as long as it stays in that niche, it's difficult to see how it could ever be a direct competitor.
>
> **The Herring:** But can't PC hardware be used to build a low cost NFS server with high reliability and performance? If so, what's the real value of Auspex's proprietary hardware platform?
>
> **Boucher:** There wouldn't be any value at all. But in reality you simply can't do what we do with PC hardware. A PC is a single-board computer and you can only get so much performance and data through a single-board computer. Until you do it in a multi-processing environment, you are still stuck with a PC.

History, of course, tells us that Auspex faded away while NetApp became the powerhouse of network-attached storage.

Enterprise Array Controllers: A More Intelligent Brain

As the storage industry moved from the late '90s into the mid '00s, the market stabilized into a smaller, more mature, set of storage system suppliers who had successfully created then defended their turf. At the same time, the enterprise array controllers from these vendors began to develop greater distinguishing characteristics.

Benefiting from even faster, more robust internal CPU and memory, enterprise array controllers began to exhibit strong and distinctly unique advanced data management software features that differentiated them from others in the storage marketplace. Such features became key differentiators between vendors. They also led to the emergence of modern-day storage system intelligence.

In 2006, Dan Warmenhoven (then NetApp's CEO), explained this emerging trend in an article from the time.

He pointed out the difference between racking up a bunch of disks to the array controller and intelligence of an enterprise storage system as follows:

> "If you're looking for cheap storage, you're talking to the wrong guy. We get asked all the time, 'How do you expect to sell disk drives at 60% gross margin?' The answer is, 'It's not about the disk. It's not about the storage. It's about the data-management services."[36]

In truth, today's enterprise storage array controller operates more like an air traffic controller at a busy metropolitan airport, safely navigating airplanes (or in our case, data packets) from a central hub, to destinations spread around the world.

In each case, the controllers are responsible for operating under often extreme loads. They are also required to orchestrate the operation of multiple concurrent activities which often originate from different regions and divisions.

Modern array controllers are responsible for processing not just key data I/O operations between hosts and disk drives, but also a wide set of emerging data management tasks running in the background. How successfully the controller performs these tasks is a key factor comprising the storage system capabilities. Table 4-2 describes many such tasks.

Table 4-2. Data Management Tasks Addressed by Modern Arrays.

Function	Description
Performance	Storage arrays are required to quickly process a multitude of data I/O requests arriving simultaneously from hundreds (or thousands) of desktops and servers.
Resiliency	Resiliency features have grown to include a variety of behind-the-scenes housekeeping functions that include: • Automated RAID Rebuilds • Data Integrity Checks (lost, misplaced or corrupt writes) • "Phone Home" Alerts • Environmental Monitoring • Non-disruptive Software Updates
Virtualization	Storage virtualization has evolved to include increasingly sophisticated storage tasks, such as: • Transparent Volume/LUN resizing • Thin Provisioning • Data Cloning • Data Compression • Data Deduplication

The Future: Controllers and the Need for Speed

Modern storage array controllers have evolved with increasingly sophisticated software payloads. This means their associated processors depend heavily on the processing speeds provided by the CPU semiconductor industry. Unfortunately, this also means that storage vendors must rely on the CPU vendor's ability to provide this additional speed, either with faster processing or with multicore CPUs.

To reduce this dependency on CPUs and to prepare for even greater innovation, storage vendors are beginning to leverage software and hardware parallelism for the future development of ever more powerful storage systems that carry out increasingly complex operations. This concept is known as *software-defined storage*, or SDS.

As with every new trend, storage vendors don't want to miss an opportunity to jump on the "software-defined" bandwagon. So, describing today's software-defined storage is a bit tricky. Storage vendors all seem to have a different idea of what it is based on the products they sell.

But, in a nutshell, SDS separates the storage controller from the storage devices. Instead of running within the storage array controller, SDS runs on one or more virtualized servers. Instead of using dedicated storage shelves, SDS data is stored on commodity disks directly connected to these servers.

One of the better-know examples of SDS is *Ceph*, a fault-tolerant, distributed, clustered, system of servers and storage devices. Many people think that Ceph-like systems represent a nirvana for modern storage: you have many servers, and each one pitches in a few disks, and then there's a filesystem that is visible to all servers in the cluster. If a server fails, that's OK – the other servers simply pick up the slack. If a disk (or SSD) fails, that's okay too, since its data is fully distributed across several servers with multiple copies available. By the way, if you see the similarity between Ceph and Amazon Dynamo (described in Chapter One), give yourself an "A" – you're paying attention! Both are variations of software-defined storage!

As demonstrated by the Amazon cloud, SDS becomes even more interesting when you start clustering thousands of servers and storage devices together into a single virtual storage pool. It's so interesting, in fact, that we'll devote an entire chapter to the concept of scale out storage.

Tomorrow's Storage Controller

As industry pundits postulate the potential future existence of 40 to 100 or more core processors on a single chip, and SDS storage clusters grow to unimaginable levels, it begs the question, "What could this mean for tomorrow's storage array controller?"

Here are a few prognoses on the subject:

- **Prognosis #1:** We see a future that increasingly involves scale out (or cloud-based) storage architectures. Market movers will be defined by storage-defined software vendors that emulate sophisticated storage controllers with highly advanced storage system functions.

- **Prognosis #2:** Traditional storage array controllers will continue to exist, but need to make better use of multicore capabilities by, first, compartmentalizing tasks (such as, encryption, deduplication, and erasure coding) into different parts of their brain, if you will.

Endnotes Referenced in Chapter 4

27 Image source: Chuck's House of VAX, courtesy Chuck McManis:
    http://www.mcmanis.com/chuck/computers/vaxen/dq132.htm.
28 Image Source: IBM Archives:
    http://www-03.ibm.com/ibm/history/exhibits/storage/storage_fifty3.html
29 http://www.bitsavers.org/pdf/cray/819_DiskControl_Sep75.pdf.
30 Image source courtesy Joe Rigdon, "Joe's On-line Multibus Circuit Board
    Guide," http://www.classiccmp.org/hp/multibus/multibus.html.
31 http://inventors.about.com/od/istartinventions/a/intergrated_circuit.htm.
32 http://www.semi.org/en/P043595.
33 http://en.wikipedia.org/wiki/Disk_array_controller.
34 http://gestaltit.com/all/tech/storage/devang/emc-symmetrix-20-years-making/.
35 "Larry Boucher Hangs Ten," Red Herring interview, July 31, 1993.
36 http://www.networkworld.com/nw200/2006/042406-nw200-netapp-
    profile.html?page=1.

Chapter Five: Without Memory, You Don't Have A Brain

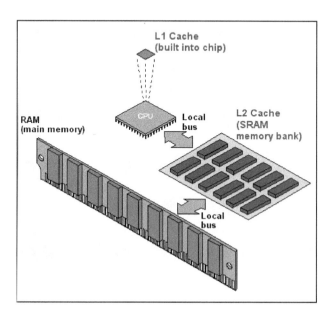

Storage systems have evolved into specialized computers. These are built to quickly and safely store and retrieve massive amounts of data. At the core, though, they are still computers. As such, they contain the same processors and memory structure of standard servers. As the diagram above illustrates, this includes the use of high speed L1 and L2 memory cache in conjunction with the CPU and a larger amount of RAM placed on the system motherboard to handle the billions of input and output requests made daily.

* * *

Memory: The Great Accelerator

In the previous chapter, we described how control of disk storage migrated over time from inside computers to inside the storage arrays themselves. This disk storage move to within the array is thanks, in large part, to the use of microprocessors and surrounding software within storage array controllers.

Now, in this chapter, we describe memory in something of a parallel evolution to that taken by disk storage.

While memory is a key component within host servers and workstations, this chapter describes how memory for storage has evolved within both the storage array and the controller itself. Much of this evolution includes the increasingly intelligent ways memory is now used to perform key storage-related tasks.

Storage System Memory and Memory in the Human Brain

The title of this chapter, "Without Memory, You Don't Have a Brain," implies the critical nature of memory within the context of an evolving, intelligent storage brain. In large part, this holds true for humans as well. Without memory, you haven't got much of the functional human intelligence most of us take for granted.

For example, without memory, simple repetitive tasks would require a great deal of human processing time. They would also result in tremendous inefficiencies. For instance, each morning, if we humans had to consult a user's guide each time we made our morning coffee, and then had to follow a detailed map each time we drove to work, we might never have found the time to invent things like gourmet coffee makers or GPS navigation systems!

To further correlate human memory and data storage memory, it may help to think of different types of human memory in much the same way as different service tiers in a storage system, where each tier of disk storage or computer memory has its own performance and capacity profile.

Human memory can be broken into three distinct categories:[37]

1. **Sensory memory.** Sensory memory occurs in the first few hundred milliseconds after you encounter an item. This allows you to look at the item and instantly remember it.

2. **Short-term memory.** Short-term memory lets you quickly recall items (an average recall capacity is 4-5 items) within several seconds after encountering them without the need to first memorize the items.

3. **Long-term memory.** Long-term memory has a potentially unlimited capacity (even to infinity) and duration (remembering items for as long as an entire lifetime) for storing larger amounts of information.

In Table 5-1, we contrast the different types of human memory with their data storage counterparts.

Table 5-1 Comparing Human Memory to Storage System Memory.

Human Memory	Storage System Memory
Sensory memory	Buffers and registers in the storage controller CPU
Short-term memory	Cache memory, Random Access Memory (RAM), flash and solid state disk (SSD)
Long-term memory	Hard disk drives

The Past: Memory is Only for Computers

The early days of computers through most of the '70s saw various memory technologies used as main memory to process and store key computer functions. In contrast, early disk storage devices and storage controllers had no memory of their own to speak of, just buffers and registers to hold the data currently being processed.

Early computer memory was the equivalent of human sensory memory. In other words, You can see and feel what you're holding in your hand, and you know what to do with it.

Let's take a brief walk back in time and look at some early computer memory technologies that shaped the future world of computers and data storage. Table 5-2 summarizes three important memory technologies, including the eras in which they were in operation.

Table 5-2. Three Significant Memory Technologies of the Past.

Era	Memory Type
'40s – '50s	Cathode Ray Tubes
'50s – '60s	Magnetic Core Memory
'70s - present	Random Access Memory (RAM) integrated circuits

Believe it or not, as the table above shows, early computer memory took the form of analog tubes, those glowing little things that powered your grandfather's radio (if your grandfather lived in the '40s, that is). The Williams Tube (or Williams-Kilburn Tube) is credited with being the first form of random access memory in the history of computing.[38]

More on the Williams Tube: The Williams-Kilburn cathode ray tube was able to store data as an electronically charged array of separate dots and dashes. The dots and dashes reflected either a '0' or '1' setting, based on the degree and frequency of charges applied to the fixed dot position. To understand exactly how this process worked, check out the detailed explanation found at the University of Manchester's Web site[39] commemorating the 50th anniversary of the birth of the modern computer. You're guaranteed to have a whole new appreciation for your grandfather's early radio!

Figure 5-1. Tom Kilburn, Holding an Example of the World's First Computer Memory Device: The Williams-Kilburn Cathode Ray Tube.

From Tubes to Core Memory

As the use of computers began to spread, separate but related inventions surrounding a new memory type, *magnetic core memory*, were pioneered by individuals such as Frederick Vieje, Dr. An Wang [later of Wang Laboratories], Way-Dong Woo, Kenneth Olson [later of DEC] and Jay Forrester.

Their separate efforts – combined with widespread mass production of core memory – would ultimately lead to the replacement of slow and somewhat unreliable tube memory by magnetic core memory.

Unlike prior memory types, core memory offered faster operation without the need to use large, expensive tubes. Magnetic core memory also proved to be an early form of non-volatile random access memory (NV-RAM). This meant it could retain its stored data even when system power was turned off. Core memory used copper wires threaded through small magnetic rings, or cores. These cores were capable of storing data bits based on the direction of magnetic field polarity the cores contained.[40]

Figure 5-2. Sample of a Magnetic Core Memory Card.[41]

Figure 5-3. Copper Wire Threaded through Magnetic Core Rings.[42]

From Core Memory to Chips

Core memory remained in use until the dawn of modern-day computers. At that point, core memory cards were replaced by integrated circuit boards which contained CPU and IC-based RAM chips.

The move away from core memory can be traced back to developments by companies like IBM who first performed ground-breaking work in the 1960s on memory cells and silicon memory chips. This work incorporated transistors and resistors. Intel ultimately came to market in 1970 with the first commercial Dynamic Random Access Memory (DRAM) chip, the Intel 1103. This was followed a few years later by the Mostek MK4096.[43]

Figure 5-4. The Intel 1103 DRAM.[44]

DRAM allowed data to be accessed randomly from its internal solid-state memory cells. It was a form of volatile memory whose contents were lost once the power was turned off. It therefore needed to be periodically refreshed. This is why it is called "Dynamic" RAM vs. its counterpart, Static RAM (SRAM). DRAM and SRAM operated directly opposite from NV-RAM. In contrast, NV-RAM operated more like earlier core memory. Its data contents remained even after power was removed.

DRAM was later grouped into single-inline memory modules (SIMMs), another Wang Laboratories innovation from the early '80s. You could plug SIMMs (and later DIMMs) directly into the motherboard of early personal computers like 286-based PCs. You could easily upgrade them with more memory. SIMMs and DIMMs formed the basis of PC main memory in the '80s and early '90s.[45] Naturally, they also found their way into the more powerful application servers.

In the most simplistic terms, DRAM, SRAM, NV-RAM, SIMMs and DIMMs were much higher capacity, much faster, and much more reliable than any prior form of system memory.

Since Intel's innovation of the 1103 DRAM in 1970, solid-state memory development has essentially followed the original Intel concept. Over the past 40 years, it has just become progressively larger, faster and cheaper.

Evolving Use of Memory for Data Storage Caching

The invention of DRAM and subsequent SIMM cards moved memory into the modern era. Companies in the '80s and early '90s could now begin to use memory in inventive ways. At this point, memory hierarchies[46] began to emerge in modern computer networks.

These hierarchies involved the distribution of memory across the entire computing infrastructure. Extensive use of memory in servers, desktops, network switches, storage systems and even printers accelerated the flow of data to all corners of the computer network.

For the world of enterprise storage, this meant that any data held in "short-term" solid state memory offered important acceleration within the server-to-storage I/O chain: Memory buffers (often referred to as memory *cache*) helped speed application workloads with heavy I/O *write* requests, while previously written data cached in memory helped speed application workloads involving heavy I/O *read* requests.

Early Write-Caching: Disk Caching vs. Journaling

One early example of write caching came from Legato Systems in 1989. The company introduced its first product, *Prestoserve*, as an NFS accelerator board intended for use with Sun-3 and Sun-4 servers.

According to one report, Prestoserve came with a large cache of memory, responsible for "buffering the NFS Server's critical filesystem state...and scheduling writes to the server's hard disks." The Prestoserve board also came with a battery backup system that could preserve data in the cache in the event of system failure or power outage.

An example that has many similarities to Legato's server-based Prestoserve was NetApp's innovative use of NV-RAM to quickly commit writes directly within a storage system.

Like Prestoserve, NetApp systems also used a battery backup to ensure data stored in memory would remain protected and preserved. Also like Prestoserve, the NetApp system focused on speeding up write processing via this memory cache.

However, unlike the Legato board, NetApp's use of NV-RAM diverged in a few key ways specific to data storage. This divergence is described in the following excerpt.

"The [NetApp] storage appliance uses battery-backed up non-volatile RAM (NVRAM) to avoid losing any data input/output requests that might have occurred after the most recent consistency point. During a normal system shutdown, the storage appliance turns off protocol services, flushes all cached operations to disk and turns off the NVRAM. When the storage appliance restarts after a system failure or power loss, it replays any protocol requests in the NVRAM that have not reached disk.

Using NVRAM to store a log of uncommitted requests is very different from using NVRAM as a disk cache, as some UNIX products do. When NVRAM is used at the disk layer, it may contain data that is critical to file system consistency. If the NVRAM fails, the file system may become inconsistent in ways that fsck cannot correct.

WAFL uses NVRAM as a file system journal, not as a cache of disk blocks that need be changed on the drives. As such, WAFL use of NVRAM space is extremely efficient. For example, a request for a file system to create a file can be described in just a few hundred bytes of information, whereas the actual operation of creating a file on disks might involve changing a dozen blocks of information or more. Because WAFL uses NVRAM as a journal of operations that need to be performed on the drives, rather than the result of the operations themselves, thousands of operations can be journaled in a typical storage appliance NVRAM log."[47]

NetApp's innovative use of NV-RAM was one of the first uses of "intelligent" memory in a storage system. It also gave credence to the company's early promise that its network-attached storage (NAS) could operate safely and perform faster than the more popular SCSI Direct-Connect Storage (DAS) of the day (this, despite the fact it had to operate across relatively slow Ethernet networks).

Looking Forward - Future Memory Technologies

Memory technologies continue to evolve. Some even suggest that large storage systems built entirely using memory (defined as Storage Class Memory, or SCM) may someday be the ultimate storage system.

One innovation gaining momentum is the Hybrid Memory Cube (HMC). This operates 15 times faster than traditional DRAMs but uses 70% less power with a 90% smaller footprint. The Hybrid Memory Cube Consortium consists of over 100 technology companies and is led by the three largest memory makers in the world.[48] Such a breadth of interest in HMC merits tracking its future progress.

Cubes that Climb Over the Memory Wall

Here's how the HMC Consortium describes the problem solved by HMC:

"Over time, memory bandwidth has become a bottleneck to system performance in high-performance computing, high-end servers, graphics, and (very soon) mid-level servers.

Conventional memory technologies are not scaling with Moore's Law; therefore, they are not keeping pace with the increasing performance demands of the latest microprocessor roadmaps. Microprocessor enablers are doubling cores and threads-per-core to greatly increase performance and workload capabilities by distributing work sets into smaller blocks and distributing them among an increasing number of work elements, i.e. cores.

Having multiple compute elements per processor requires an increasing amount of memory per element. This results in a greater need for both memory bandwidth and memory density to be tightly coupled to a processor to address these challenges. The term 'memory wall' has been used to describe this dilemma."[49]

HMC products first began to ship in 2014[50]. Although primarily used in supercomputers today, many feel that HMC will eventually work its way down to traditional corporate servers with its promise to accelerate multicore CPU applications with near-zero latencies and the ability to process billions of memory operations per second![51]

When you look at memory's journey—from the emergence of the cathode ray tube in the '40s to tomorrow's potential hybrid memory cube—it's clear to see how profoundly memory and caching technologies have evolved.

Given the increasing pace at which technological innovation now occurs and the ever-present quest to reduce latency and speed operational efficiency, We have no doubt of the continued emergence of other memory breakthroughs (including those not yet on the industry radar).

In conjunction with these breakthroughs, we can also expect to see today's storage system vendors innovating in the ways they use memory.

As a matter of fact, this brings us to the next chapter, where we describe a few such innovative uses of memory in storage. Just keep reading if you're ready to flash forward. . .

Endnotes Referenced in Chapter 5

37 http://en.wikipedia.org/wiki/Memory.
38 http://en.wikipedia.org/wiki/Williams_tube.
39 http://www.computer50.org/kgill/williams/williams.html#change.
40 http://en.wikipedia.org/wiki/Core_memory.
41 Image source: http://www.nzeldes.com/HOC/images/CoreMemory01.jpg.
    Image courtesy Nathan Zeldes, http://www.nzeldes.com.
42 Image is also courtesy Nathan Zeldes,
    http://www.nzeldes.com/HOC/images/CoreMemory03.jpg.
43 http://en.wikipedia.org/wiki/DRAM.
44 http://www.cpu-museum.net/.
45 http://en.wikipedia.org/wiki/SIMM.
46 http://www.real-knowledge.com/memory.htm.
47 http://media.netapp.com/documents/tr-3001.pdf.
48 http://www.hybridmemorycube.org/.
49 http://www.hybridmemorycube.org/faq.html#problem.
50 http://www.pcworld.com/article/2366680/computer-memory-overhaul-due-
    with-microns-hmc-in-early-2015.html
51 http://www.hotchips.org/wp-content/uploads/hc_archives/hc23/HC23.18.3-
    memory-FPGA/HC23.18.320-HybridCube-Pawlowski-Micron.pdf.

***

Chapter Six: Flash Forward

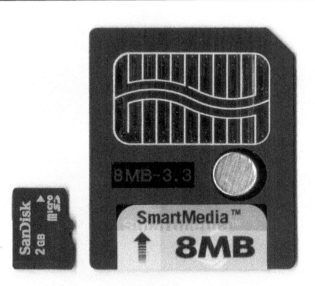

The right side of the above image shows Toshiba's original, 1995-era SmartMedia 8MB flash module, originally known as a Solid State Floppy Disk Card (SSFDC). Compare the size difference between this much larger SSFDC card and it's more recent, 2GB flash counterpart (SanDisk example shown at left). This smaller flash card is known as an SDXC card (based on the Secure Digital eXtended Capacity, or SDXC, format it uses). With capacities as high as 256GB,[52] today's SDXC cards represent a 32,000X capacity improvement over Toshiba's original flash design some 18 years earlier.

***

Pre-Flash and the Need For Faster Long-Term Memory

As we discussed in the previous chapter, memory is an integral part of the design of data storage systems. To a large extent, these systems could be thought of as the long-term memory bank for all of IT. Similar to the human brain's long-term memory bank, in this case, storage systems are designed to remember every piece of information entering the data center.

While short-term memory is held on a server's or storage controller's DRAM, for decades longer term memory has been held on the disk drives themselves. The great thing about disk drives is that they store a lot of information for a relatively low cost. The not-so-great thing about them, however, is that they are much, much, slower than DRAM at delivering this information when needed.

Attempts to Close the "Fast DRAM/Slower Disk" Gap

Over the years, many attempts were made to fill the gap between slow disk drives and fast DRAM used by CPUs. We'll describe a few of the most notable efforts here, which include:

- Short stroking
- Interleaving
- Lower cost memory adjuncts to DRAM

For various reasons, however, you'll soon see why each of these efforts invariably fell short.

Attempt #1: Short Stroking

A common method used to close the gap between fast DRAM and slower disk was to partially fill the drives so that stored data would be contained in a relatively small area on the drive. This practice, known as short stroking,[53] kept data on only the outermost disk cylinders.

Although this practice is still in use today, there remain pros and cons to this approach:

Pros: Improves disk drive performance by limiting the movement of the read/write heads.

Cons: Reduces the amount of data that can be stored on each disk drive.

> **Data Storage and Racing Engines.** The term, short stroking, was actually borrowed from the auto racing industry. Here, it refers to increasing the performance of a piston-driven engine.[54]

Attempt #2: Interleaving

Another technique to improve disk performance was to simultaneously stripe data chunks across several parallel disk drives. This idea, also known as interleaving,[55] was based on the following premise:

If: You synchronized the platter rotation of a bank of disk drives (which could then, in turn, read and write the data simultaneously)

Then: You could improve disk performance by a factor of n (where n is the number of disk drives in the bank).

Today, while some forms of RAID—notably RAID-4—do take advantage of non-synchronized disk striping, the practice of interleaving has also been met with its own share of pros and cons:

Pros: Significantly improves disk drive performance by reading and writing data in larger "chunks".

Cons: Too difficult for drive vendors to precisely synchronize disk drive spindles. For this reason, the practice of synchronized interleaving has been largely abandoned.

Attempt #3: Other Low-Cost Memory Options

The same time that attempts were being made to improve disk performance, work was also being done to provide a lower cost, non-volatile memory module for use in conjunction with DRAM. Perhaps the most infamous was bubble memory, described below:

> "Before hard disks took over as the dominant form of computer storage, Andrew Bobeck created what was supposed to be the next big thing: Bubble memory. Comprised of a thin film of magnetized material that would store one bit of data in in little domains called bubbles, Bobeck's memory was seen as the next big thing. Large companies like Bell Labs, Konami (which released an arcade system based around the memory), and even Intel invested in research. However, when the hard disk arrived with faster data speeds, more storage, and a cheaper production cost, all work on Bobeck's baby came to a halt."[56]

Other attempts to design a product with DRAM speeds and disk drive costs have included:

- Magnetic RAM (MRAM)
- Phase-change RAM (PCRAM)
- Resistive RAM (RRAM)
- Ferro-electric RAM (FRAM)

These attempts have also had their pros and cons:

Pros: More reliable than disk drives (due to no moving parts).

Cons: Various problems experienced with scalability, performance or high manufacturing cost have precluded these products from reaching the market.

Despite their promise, the problems associated with alternative DRAM technologies proved so insurmountable that the technologies thus far have failed to succeed.

. . . And Then There Was Flash

The start of the 2000s saw a huge rise (and correlated drop in sticker prices) of consumer products that required miniature storage devices. This was especially true for video recorders, digital cameras, and MP3 players which relied on small and cheap storage.

This section briefly chronicles the evolution of various technologies used to store data for the emerging field of consumer digital playback/recording products. These include:

- Micro disk drives
- Early flash

Early suppliers of these consumer products first used tiny, one-inch "micro" disk drives to store these large files.

Then, thanks to work done in the 1980s by Dr. Fujio Masuoka at Toshiba, a new solution appeared: flash memory.

How Flash Got its Name: One source reports the following, "Flash memory (both NOR and NAND types) was invented by Dr. Fujio Masuoka while working for Toshiba circa 1980. According to Toshiba, the name 'flash' was suggested by Dr. Masuoka's colleague, Mr. Shoji Ariizumi, because the erasure process of the memory contents reminded him of the flash of a camera."

Flash brought new innovation in a standard, packaged module. Suddenly, flash offered a plug-and-play replacement for the aforementioned micro disk-drives.

Another key to the success of flash was its ability to erase and re-record single memory cells. This was in direct contrast to earlier EEPROMs which needed to be completely erased before any new data could be written.

The rest, as they say, is history. Consumer demand took off. Prices plummeted. Flash has since become the de facto standard for storage within these new devices, which now includes smart phones and tablets. It's safe to say that that these products would not even exist today without Dr. Masuoka's flash invention.

> **Did You Know?** For his pioneering work on flash memory, Masuoka has received numerous honors and awards including the Gift of Watanabe Japanese prime minister in 1977 and the National Invention Award in 1980. In 2007, Masuoka was awarded the Purple Ribbon Medal from Emperor Akihito.

For all its greatness, however, flash has also had its share of pros and two acknowledged cons (or weaknesses). These include:

Pros: Plug-and-play module with memory cells that can be easily erased, then re-recorded.

Cons: Failure due to multiple erasures over time.

(Like all forms of EEPROM, those little transistors inside the memory module don't like being flashed. Eventually, after multitudes of electrical erasures, the transistor gates start to break down and will eventually fail.)

Another con is that flash, typically known for its speed, can sometimes be slower than disk due to the constant need to first erase contents before writing.

Flash to the Future

To counter the two, acknowledged weaknesses of flash—failure caused by multiple erasures and slow speeds during certain operations—we have begun to see some interesting innovation in the areas of flash technology.

For instance, SLC (Single-level Cell) flash has traditionally been used in demanding environments as it offers 10X durability over cheaper, consumer-grade MLC (Multi-level Cell) flash. But, its high costs have caused flash manufacturers to look at other forms of flash:

- **eMLC.** To combat the higher costs of SLC flash and bring lower cost flash into play for demanding applications, companies are now offering MLC flash with sophisticated wear-leveling and bad block management (BBM) algorithms.. These products have become known as eMLC (e for *enterprise*) devices. eMLC also contains some slight tweaking of the flash erasure cycles for increased durability.

- **TLC.** The latest entrant into the flash cell wars is TLC (triple-level cell), which offers dramatically higher flash capacities and lower costs. The downside, however, is that TLC also offers slower access times and lower reliability than even MLC flash.

Will TLC flash make its way into the enterprise? My guess is yes. Expect to see storage pattern algorithms becoming even more sophisticated, with similar increases in durability.

Flash in the Evolution of Data Storage

Despite its start in consumer-based products, flash has been an important evolutionary step in storage technology.

The enterprise storage industry first watched the use of flash memory explode in consumer markets. It also saw the resulting economies of scale that drove down costs. Not much time elapsed before these vendors also began to explore how flash technology could be used in intelligent storage systems as a means to further accelerate performance.

Jumping on the Flash Bandwagon

Every once in a while, a technology comes along that revolutionizes the way we store enterprise data. Flash is on the verge of becoming one of those technologies. Every major storage vendor has now incorporated some form of flash-based technology into their architecture.

In contrast to the compact flash modules common in consumer products, flash tends to take on two forms in the enterprise:

- **PCIe (Peripheral Component Interconnect Express) cards** that plug into standard slots in servers and storage controllers
- **SSDs (solid state drives)** that look and feel just like traditional disk drives but are entirely silicon-based (and thus have no moving parts)

Here, implementations of flash by storage vendors tend to vary widely. An analogy could be made to the early days of aviation. From the Wright Brothers' first flight until the mass-produced airplanes of WWII, aircraft designs took on all sorts of experimental shapes and sizes until finally standardizing on the single-wing design we are all familiar with today. As with any new and popular technology, flash vendors are still experimenting with various design approaches.

The Many Flavors of Flash in Storage

Some vendors have opted to deploy flash-based PCIe cards and/or SSDs as their own 'Tier 0' within an existing storage array cabinet. These storage systems, known as hybrid storage arrays, combine flash devices with management software. Their intended goal? To automatically migrate data between solid state disk and magnetic (hard disk) storage tiers based on performance needs.

Other vendors have designed entire storage systems containing only flash devices with no magnetic storage whatsoever.

To help you gain a broader understanding of the different methods (and applications) for using flash with storage systems, I'll use my own knowledge of NetApp storage as the backdrop for a few, real-world use case examples.

NetApp has embraced the widespread use of flash technologies in three distinct ways:

1. Flash as cache in the storage system
2. SSD as cache in the storage system
3. SSD as disk in the storage system

Since these categories encompass the major ways that flash is used today by many storage vendors, I'll describe each use case in the next few sections.

Use Case #1: Flash as Cache in the Storage System

NetApp *Flash Cache* is an example of flash being used as cache in the storage system.

NetApp Flash Cache is a line of flash-based PCIe cards that plug directly into the storage controller slots. It is used to improve performance of read-intensive workloads. Flash Cache is meant to improve performance by offering an additional caching layer and special tiering software. The tiering software is responsible for automatically promoting hot data from disk drives to flash.

Designed purely for speed, Flash Cache employs many techniques to automatically improve performance. These include intelligent interleaving of writes in order to create balanced erase, write, and read cycles.

Since each flash write requires a slow erasure cycle, it's best to have as many cycles as possible running in parallel to maintain throughput.

Use Case #2: SSD as Cache in the Storage System

NetApp *Flash Pool* is an example of using SSD as cache in the storage system itself. In this case, NetApp Flash Pool combines SSDs with disk drives in a "hybrid" storage system. Such a hybrid arrangement allows these systems to take advantage of SSDs' low-latency and high-throughput benefits, while maintaining the mass storage capacity of disk drives.

Using a combination of SSD and disk drives within a single pool allows data to be automatically placed on the proper storage medium for optimal performance. Like Flash Cache, NetApp Flash Pool functionality does not move hot data to SSD. Rather, a copy of the data is created in SSD.

Why Copy Data Instead of Just Moving it to SSD?

Copying rather than moving data has the following benefits:

- **Speed due to less steps.** Copying data is a faster I/O process than moving it. Moving it requires more time-consuming steps: The system has to copy the data, verify the copy, and then delete it from its original location.
- **Speed due to less data rewrites to disk.** Once the hot data is ejected from the SSD, copying means there is now no need to rewrite the data back to disk. Why, you ask? Because it's already there!

Unlike Flash Cache, both reads and writes can be cached in NetApp Flash Pool SSDs. Why is this important? This relates to our earlier mention of a few situations—such as sequential write operations—when disk drives can actually outperform SSDs.

With a Flash Pool-enabled system, Flash Pool logic allows the storage system to make the best decision about how to treat read or write operations. For example, when a write operation occurs, Flash Pool logic determines whether it's faster to write to SSD and disk together or just straight to disk. Conversely, when a read operation occurs, Flash Pool logic determines whether data should be cached to SSD or read directly from disk without caching.

How does Flash Pool logic make this determination? It's based primarily on whether the data pattern is random or sequential. In all cases, Flash Pool algorithms are optimized for speed.

Use Case #3: SSD as Disk in the Storage System

Some workloads can justify the use of all flash, all the time. NetApp *All-flash FAS* is an all-flash array that serves this purpose. Properly constructed flash arrays can mask the inherent weaknesses of flash in a few different ways:

- **Combating flash memory wear-out.**[57] Cell wear-out can be a real problem, particularly when flash is being used to store critical data. To combat this issue, all-flash arrays contain the same RAID protection as traditional disk-based storage systems. In this case, if a flash cell fails, the data it contained can be recovered by the remaining cells.

- **Combating flash memory write cliffs.**[58] As we've previously mentioned, the erase cycle of flash is very long in CPU terms. For write-intense situations, this creates the possibility of a flash write cliff. Write cliffs occur when all cells are busy erasing and, therefore, can't accept new data to write. To avoid this, all-flash arrays use

> sophisticated cell mapping and NVRAM data staging to
> ensure that flash cells are always available for writing.

So Many Flash Choices. . .How to Decide?

The prior use case examples of flash in storage can
sometimes create a quandary for users: How do they
know which implementation is best for them? Table 6-1
can help you determine the best application fit for each
use case.

Table 6-1. When to Use Different Types of Flash for Storage.

Flash Use Case:	Pros & Cons:	When to Use:
Storage Array Cache *(i.e. NetApp Flash Cache)*	**Pros:** Automatic caching of all hot data in storage system **Cons:** Limited capacity	When a small percentage of data requires very fast access.
Hybrid Storage System *(i.e. NetApp Flash Pool)*	**Pros:** Increased read cache capacity + write cache **Cons:** Higher cost	In larger storage systems requiring greater amounts of cache.
All-Flash Array *(i.e. NetApp All-flash FAS)*	**Pros:** All data always stored on flash **Cons:** Highest cost	When a dedicated storage system is needed for a critical application

In truth, a combination of the above will likely be
deployed in the typical data center. For example, a high-
speed transactional database might employ both an all-
flash array while more mundane applications, such as
MRP, might employ storage array cache.

The Future: A Flash In The Pan?

As predicted in my earlier book, flash has become one of the most interesting technologies to come along in some time. We've since seen it enter every corner of the storage industry. However, despite the enthusiasm for the benefits of flash technology, many industry analysts, vendors and experts question whether or not flash will be the long-term technology choice of solid state storage. Many (although far fewer these days) also question whether flash will eventually replace disk drives. Among today's questions: Will there be one dominant architecture or multiple?[59]

Many experts don't believe that flash will be part of the long-term success of SSDs. New solid-state memory technologies should ultimately prove more viable for SSD design. Today, the race to replace flash seems to have settled into four distinct camps[60], as described in Table 6-2:

Table 6-2. Potential Replacements for Flash Memory.

Technology	Description
Memristor	The concept of memristor, short for memory resistor, has been around since the early 1970s, thanks to predictions made by then-professor Leon Chua at the University of California at Berkeley.
	Memristor is a form of non-volatile memory that acts as a newer, fourth building block in electrical circuits, next to its earlier cousins (capacitors, resistors and inductors). Different from a traditional resistor, a memristor doesn't just safely flow current across a device, but is capable of remembering its charges even after power loss, letting it store information. HP Labs proved the theory of memristors in 2008 when it created a working prototype. Whether or not memristors will ever see the light of day is anyone's guess, but there is evidence that substantial research is

Technology	Description
	ongoing[61].
Phase Change Memory (PCM)	PCM has been touted and studied in-depth for the past several years as one emerging, highly viable alternative to flash memory.
	According to UCSD researchers who demonstrated the technology on the university's Moneta system back in 2011, PCM "stores data in the glass-like structure of a metal alloy called chalcogenide that changes states as atoms are rearranged."[62] Back then, researchers noted these benefits:
	No moving parts (similar to flash)
	Thousands of times speed improvements over a conventional hard drive
	Up to seven times speed improvements over flash drives
	Throughput speeds as high as 1.1GB per second when reading large data quantities
	(Besides Intel, other vendors working on PCM include Micron, Samsung and IBM.)
Magneto-resistive random access memory (MRAM)	Heralded in some circles as a "universal memory" and a natural heir to flash and other forms of non-volatile random access memory, one version of MRAM called *Spin Torque Transfer* is a technique that polarizes the electrons (spin-aligns them) in the various layers (or magnetic domain walls) of a RAM chip.
	Based on this polarization, a "torque" can be transferred to a nearby chip layer. The result, sometimes known as "racetrack memory," lowers the current required to write to the cells, thus making it similar to the current needed to read from them.[63]
	A few years back, IBM prototyped STT-MRAM with early plans to include it in future storage arrays.[64] Since then, other emerging companies have entered the field of STT-MRAM.[65] Western Digital's Hitachi Global Storage Technologies has also been pursuing a differentiated offshoot of

Technology	Description
	STT with UCLA researchers, called MeRAM (Magneto-electric RAM), with promising results.[66]
	(Note: STT-MRAM technology is called, interchangeably, either spin-torque-transfer or spin-transfer-torque.)
3D xPoint (Crosspoint)	Is Crosspoint memory a form of Phase Change Memory? Or is it based on Magneto Resistive RAM? No one seems to really know, and the vendors aren't talking. All we know for sure is that Intel and Micron jointly announced this technology in 2015, with shipments promised in 2017. Crosspoint memory seems to address all of the key requirements that close the gap between DRAM and flash with 1000x faster performance and 1000x more endurance than NAND flash, and 10x the density of DRAM, and the icing on the cake is that this new technology is non-volatile, just like flash. Intel is using the name for its products *Optane* while Micron uses the name *QuantX.* Pricing is expected to be ½ the price of DRAM, and 4X-5X the price of flash, putting Crosspoint in the crosshairs of a very interesting price/performance target.

Predictions, Prognoses and Other Interesting Developments

Just as SSD vendors continue to reduce costs and improve reliability, we'll continue to see disk drive vendors chugging along with a proven formula and ever-increasing capacities.

In 2012 alone, Seagate announced plans to produce an HAMR 60TB disk sometime before 2022.[67] Capacities like this will make it awfully hard for flash-based (or PCM, Memristor, or MRAM-based) SSD vendors to keep pace. As such, we don't expect to see a major cross-over occurring between disk drives and SSD for another 5 years (or, perhaps, 10 years at the most).

In the meantime, we'll continue to see flash and SSD technologies implemented tactically:

As an accelerant in traditional storage systems
(or)
In small capacity (purpose-built for high performance) all-flash storage arrays

Within five years, we would expect to see flash being replaced by a new (and better) solid-state memory technology, likely one of those I've mentioned above.

At least, that's the way we see it. How about you?

Endnotes Referenced in Chapter 6

52 http://www.lexar.com/products/sdhc-sdxc-memory-cards.
53 http://en.wikipedia.org/wiki/Disk_partitioning.
54 http://www.howstuffworks.com/question381.htm.
55 http://en.wikipedia.org/wiki/Interleaving.
56 http://www.complex.com/tech/2012/10/10-technologies-that-were-supposed-to-blow-but-never-did/bubble-memory.
57. http://searchsolidstatestorage.techtarget.com/definition/NAND-flash-wear-out.
58 http://storagemojo.com/2012/06/07/the-ssd-write-cliff-in-real-life/.
59 http://dcsblog.burtongroup.com/data_center_strategies/2008/07/ssd---storage-i.html and
    http://media.techtarget.com/searchStorage/downloads/StoragemagOnlineSept 2009.pdf.
60 http://www.tomshardware.com/news/ibm-pcm-tlc-3d-xpoint,31811.html.
61 https://www.youtube.com/watch?v=3OAJr-2ljNc.
62 http://www.macworld.com/article/1160266/phasechangememory.html.
63 http://en.wikipedia.org/wiki/Magnetoresistive_random-access_memory.
64 http://www-03.ibm.com/press/us/en/pressrelease/23859.wss.
65 http://www.spintransfer.com/news-events/spin-transfer-technologies-names-dr-mustafa-pinarbasi-chief-technology-officer.php.
66 http://semimd.com/blog/tag/stt-ram/.
67 http://www.computerworld.com/s/article/9225335/With_tech_breakthrough_Sea gate_promises_60TB_drives_this_decade.

Chapter Seven: The Storage Nervous System

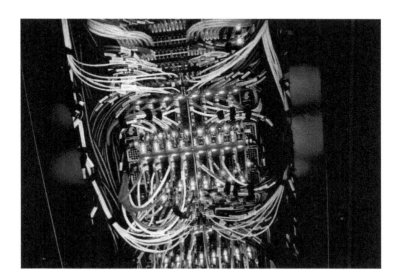

The Gordon Compute Cluster, pictured above, is a unique, data-intense supercomputer housed at the University of California - San Diego Supercomputer Center (SDSC).[68] Gordon (as in *Flash Gordon*) was designed as a research platform for High Performance Computing (HPC) environments. It contains 64TB of DRAM, 300TB of flash storage, and 1.5PB of traditional disk storage. Capable of 35 million input/output instructions per second (IOPS), scientists have used Gordon for complex data analysis. One example is its use in identifying a gene-expression process in the human brain that could aid in the development of future treatments for mental conditions like schizophrenia or autism-spectrum disorders.[69]

* * *

Storage: A Sophisticated Neural Network

This chapter covers the central nervous system associated with data storage systems. While some may guess at the functions of this nervous system, I'll offer a comparative analogy comparing storage to the human brain's central nervous system.

Some people liken the role of the human central nervous system to an "information control" center and neural net that receives and responds to both internal and external stimuli.[70]

A storage system's nervous system is similar in its need to receive and respond to both internal and external information. It needs to process information coming from within its own world as well as information coming from its external connections to the world.

To keep things simple, you can think of storage systems as needing to simultaneously:

- Communicate with the outside world
- Exchange information with internal components

In this chapter, first we'll discuss Item #1 above: How a modern storage system communicates with the outside world via its sophisticated storage nervous system. Later in this chapter, we'll also touch on the second part of the storage system communication equation: The ways storage systems have evolved to communicate with their own internal world.

Communicating with the Outside World

As we've discussed a few times throughout the book, communications between the storage controller and the computer system evolved from IBM's original concept of bus-and-tag cabling. Later disk drive interfaces that used adaptations of this bus-and-tag concept included:

- The Storage Module Device (SMD) interface from Control Data Corporation.[71]

- The ST-506 interface from Shugart Technology (then Seagate) associated with the first 5.25-inch hard disk drive.[72]

- The Enhanced Small Disk Interface (ESDI) from Maxtor.

> **A Walk through History with ESDI:** ESDI is one example of an early 1980s communications interface which had an interestingly popular, albeit relatively short run.[73]

Eventually, however, all these primitive storage interfaces were trumped by SCSI.

This was the dawn of direct-attached storage (DAS) systems. But, as you'll see in Table 7-1, such DAS system interfaces (like SCSI and its predecessors) still had a few challenges. Such challenges would lead to their ultimate replacement by storage systems supported by their own storage networks.

Table 7-1. Issues with DAS and Early Disk Communications Interfaces.

Challenge	Description
Restricted flexibility	Early data storage interfaces were tethered to their computer by big, fat cables. This was the start of direct-attached storage (DAS). Having storage attached to a server via umbilical cord was convenient and fast, but also very inflexible. SCSI "daisy chains" could support just 8 or 16 drives. To add or remove drives required shutdown of the entire computer system and its storage devices (a practically unthinkable scenario today).
Inability to share resources	Storage also couldn't be shared between systems. In effect, early computers said, "What's mine is mine, what's yours is yours and there will be no sharing here!" This was a big waste of unused disk capacity.

Moving External Communications onto a Storage Network

The '80s and '90s brought further proliferation of open systems and servers. It also brought more attention to the growing inefficiencies of direct-attached storage.

This led to the development of storage networks and the near-simultaneous release of two of the predominant storage networking topologies still in existence today:

- Storage area networks (SAN)
- Network-attached storage (NAS)

To the uninitiated, the SAN and NAS acronyms may sound like they describe exactly the same thing. To add to the confusion, they even spell out each other when the letters are reversed.

In reality, however, these two acronyms have some very important distinctions.

The next few sections will cover the similarities and differences between these two storage networking standards.

People are often confused by the differences between SAN and NAS. Hopefully, a few simple definitions and examples can help clear up the confusion. We'll cover the following here:

- Understanding which type of data a SAN or NAS system is designed to store.
- Understanding the various network storage communication protocols used by the SAN or NAS system to send and receive data.

To start, here are a few common distinctions you may hear in regards to SAN or NAS:

> "SAN is block-based storage while NAS is file-based storage."
>
> "NAS has its own file system and can be used as a direct file share by client workstations or hosts, while SAN relies on a server-based or host-based file system and host-based applications to fully utilize the block data it stores."

Both of these are true, yet definitions like this are confusing.

In a nutshell, here's how I explain SAN storage:

> A SAN storage system emulates disk drives, which are also known as LUNs (Logical Unit Numbers). LUNs are created by the SAN storage system. Application servers format these LUNs and turn them into usable data.

Let's take this definition a bit further. If you have a SAN storage system, you create a "virtual" LUN and export it over your storage network to a single server. The reason we call this a virtual LUN is because the SAN storage system can take many small physical disk drives and make them appear as though they are one large "virtual" disk drive.

The server then uses the same storage network to "see" my LUN, which it recognizes as its very own personal disk drive (in other words, seeing it just as if the disk were direct-attached via SCSI cable to the server).

It is now up to the server to format the LUN's raw data blocks into something usable. This is why SAN devices are commonly called "block" storage devices.

Now let's take a look at NAS storage. This is how I explain it:

> A NAS storage system emulates a file system. In other words, it represents a disk drive that has already been formatted and can be used to store data files immediately.

Here's an example of NAS in operation. If you have a NAS storage device, you create a "virtual" file system and export it onto an existing TCP/IP-based server network. The reason we call this a virtual file system is because the NAS storage system can take many small physical disk drives and make them appear as though they are one large "virtual" file system.

All the servers on the network can "see" this new file system and are free to read and write files to and from the NAS file system. This is why NAS devices are often referred to as "file" storage devices.

SAN and NAS: The Tale of Two Questions

Now that we've given you some brief definitions and examples of SAN and NAS in operation, I'd like to tackle a few common questions about SAN and NAS that leave newcomers to storage somewhat perplexed:

- Why there are two storage networks (SAN and NAS) at all.
- How five separate communication protocols evolved for storage networks.

Why Have Two Storage Networks (Both SAN and NAS)?

We'll go into more detail shortly, but the simple answer as to why we need both SAN and NAS falls under the category of performance versus convenience.

By presenting "raw" storage to the application server, SAN storage systems eliminate the middle man – therefore overhead is reduced and performance increases.

File-based NAS storage takes a few extra steps in packaging the storage to the servers. The NAS "ready-to-use" storage provides a great deal more convenience, but requires a few extra layers of translation between the servers and the underlying disk drives. This can potentially reduce performance.

How Did Five Different Storage Network Protocols Evolve?

Now let's move onto the second aspect of external SAN/NAS communications: Namely, the storage network communications protocol used to send and receive data and why there are so many of them.

To start, Table 7-2 offers an overview of the main protocols now in use with SAN or NAS storage.

Table 7-2. Popular Storage Network Protocols for SAN or NAS.

NAS Communication Protocols	
Protocol	**Description**
NFS	NFS stands for the *Network File System* protocol used by UNIX-based clients or servers. NAS systems that support the NFS protocol offer file access and file storage services to UNIX clients or servers.
CIFS/ SMB	CIFS stands for *Common Internet File System*. CIFS is another network-based protocol used for file access communications between Microsoft Windows clients and servers. CIFS actually originated from *Server Message Block* (SMB), an earlier Microsoft protocol. The two terms can be used interchangeably.[74] NAS systems supporting the CIFS protocol offer file access and file storage services to Microsoft clients and servers.
SAN Communication Protocols	
Fibre Channel Protocol	*Fibre Channel Protocol* (FCP) is an I/O interconnect protocol that allows SAN systems to send and receive block-related data between the SAN storage system and its hosts. FCP encapsulates SCSI within Fibre Channel frames. Transmission of frames typically occurs via specialized Fibre Channel cabling, Fibre Channel host bus adapters (HBAs) and Fibre Channel switches operating between the SAN and its hosts. SANs that use Fibre Channel protocol are often referred to as Fibre Channel SANs or FC SANs.
iSCSI	iSCSI stands for *Internet Small Computer Systems Interface*. According to SNIA, iSCSI is "a transport protocol that provides for the SCSI protocol to be carried over a TCP-based IP network."[75] Another way to say it is that iSCSI encapsulates SCSI within TC/IP packets. Since it uses TCP/IP as its transport network, a SAN using iSCSI is often referred to as an IP SAN.
FCoE	FCoE stands for *Fibre Channel over Ethernet*. A derivative of FCP above, FCoE allows Fibre Channel storage traffic to be sent over Ethernet networks, as opposed to specialized Fibre Channel networks. In other words, FCoE encapsulates FC frames (which, in turn, encapsulate SCSI) in TC/IP packets.

Allow me to answer the question most of you are undoubtedly asking at this point: "It seems very confusing to have both block-based and file-based storage *and* five different communications protocols! Can't this be easier?"

Like most of the topics in this book, in order to answer this question, we need to look back at history. What you'll find is an early heritage that evolved in separate paths, with growing confusion...

In the '90s, when NAS and SAN storage systems were emerging, TCP/IP networks used by servers were very slow by today's standards. 10-Megabit per second (Mbps) Ethernet was the norm, with 100-Mbps Ethernet just emerging. This was the best available network transport speed you could get back then.

In contrast, SANs came out of the gate with fiber optic cables and a protocol that could move data at 1 Gigabit per second (Gbps), a ten-fold improvement over the fastest Ethernet-based NAS transport. Also, as mentioned earlier, the protocol stack of Fibre Channel SAN had less processing overhead than the TCP/IP protocol used by NAS. This allowed FC SANs to offer potentially higher speeds.

So, in those days, anyone with a "need for speed" simply had to use SAN storage. Databases, transaction processing, analytics, and similar applications fell into this category. NAS, although less costly and easier to implement than SAN, was usually relegated to "slower" applications like user files, images and Web content.

Warning: Geek Alert! Arbitrated Loop, Packet Collisions

Fibre Channel SANs use strict protocols known as "Arbitrated Loop" and "Switched Fabric." This means the data sender and data recipient must both acknowledge they are ready to send and receive data before any data is actually sent. In a loop configuration, devices not sending or receiving data must stay off the loop during data transfers. This is often referred to as FC-AL.[76]

On the other hand, TCP/IP Ethernet (used by NAS) can be something of a traffic free-for-all. Ethernet data packets are sent and received over the network, willy-nilly, without any prior permission. This means packet "collisions" are common. Fortunately, Ethernet is known as a "Collision Detect" topology. When a packet collision does occur, an electrical spike is detected on the line by all devices. This prompts them to cease communication until the spike subsides. The offending packets are then re-sent and life resumes as normal on the network (at least until the next collision).[77]

New Realities Point to SAN/NAS Convergence & Unification

Leaving much of the confusion and separate paths of the '80s and '90s behind, much has changed over the past 20 years in the world of SAN and NAS communications.

Server TCP/IP networks have grown faster. 10-Gigabit Ethernet (10-GbE or 10 Gbps) is common in today's data centers. Even 40-Gigbit and 100-Gigabit Ethernet devices are just now being delivered.[78]

Fibre Channel SAN networks have also become faster, albeit at a slower pace. Fibre Channel networks operating at 8-Gbps are common today, with 16-Gbps having also been newly delivered. The industry is even preparing for 32-Gbps standardization.[79]

Due to the slower pace of growth for Fibre Channel SAN speeds, FC SANs no longer have the performance advantage they once had over NAS. The related increase in transport speeds now possible with Gigabit Ethernet has since prompted a few trends associated with reducing storage system complexity and simplifying the data center. These include:

- **Unifying block and file data transport onto the same network fabric.** The modern-day storage network has begun to see an increasing trend to consolidate and converge the two network storage architectures onto a single network transport fabric. Some people refer to this move as "one wire."[80] Cisco Systems is a key proponent of this trend with the company's support of a unified network fabric that incorporates the Cisco Nexus family of products with Converged Network Adapters, or CNAs.[81]

- **Unifying SAN and NAS data storage functionality onto the same storage system.** Proponents of this approach include NetApp with its unified storage architecture. This architecture supports all SAN/NAS protocols (including Fibre Channel and IP storage) from within the same storage system.[82]

These trends toward unification and convergence point to a simpler data center where management of the overall environment can become a conceivably much easier affair.

Feeling comfortable with the concepts behind of SAN and NAS? Well, get ready, because a new, emerging protocol may replace them both: *Object Storage* is gaining popularity, particularly amongst cloud storage providers. Fear not, we'll take a closer look at Object Storage in the next chapter; *It's the Efficiency, Stupid.*

Communicating with an Internal World

In this chapter, we've discussed how storage systems evolved their communications with the outside world. This includes their corresponding architectural moves from DAS to NAS, SAN and unified architectures.

Now, I'd like to briefly take on the other side of the communication equation: Communication with internal disk drives and SSDs.

Every modern enterprise storage system consists of a storage controller (or controllers), storage devices, and all the associated cables and adapter cards that cobble everything together. Drives and controllers are brought together using fiber-optic cables with high performance backplanes to ensure the cleanest, most reliable signals possible. Some systems even carry a redundant set of cables—from controllers to storage devices—to safeguard this vital connection.

These components truly represent the backbone of the storage system. They thus represent the critical, internal nervous system of the storage brain as well.

The New "Insider" Role of the Storage Controller

While the storage controller responds to data requests from the outside world using various protocols, it's also charged with a myriad of other internal tasks. These include:

- Deciding the best place to store data, based on performance needs, protection procedures, and security policies.
- Commanding internal devices to store and retrieve data in an orderly fashion
- Monitoring the status and health of its internal devices and taking any steps necessary to keep the storage system up and running

With an ever-increasing variety of internal devices, each with varying performance and costs, the storage controller not only must decide where to store its data. It must also balance the trade-offs between high performance and high costs.

How does storage intelligence play into this balancing act? This is something we touched on in the last chapter: Using the intelligence of the storage controller to automatically place data in the right place at the right time.

To demonstrate the need for storage intelligence, Table 7-3 shows how things can get complicated rather quickly.

In this example, let's assume we have a storage system with 15 adjustable storage features. Each feature has three configuration settings within it.

Table 7-3. Storage Configuration Choices and Complexities.

15 Sample Storage Features	3 Configuration Options Per Feature		
	(A) Minimal Setting	(B) Moderate Setting	(C) Maximum Setting
Sample Capacity Features:			
1. Clustered Storage Pools			✓
2. Volume Autogrow	✓		
3. Thin Provisioning		✓	
Sample Efficiency Features:			
4. Deduplication			✓
5. Snapshots		✓	
6. Data Compression	✓		

Table 7-3 (Continued).

15 Sample Storage Features (con't)	3 Configuration Options Per Feature		
	(A) Minimal Setting	(B) Moderate Setting	(C) Maximum Setting
Sample Performance Features:			
7. Automatic Load Balancing	✓		
8. Caching of Hot Data			✓
9. SSD/HDD Storage Tiering			✓
Sample Protection Features:			
10. Remote Replication		✓	
11. RAID Mirroring	✓		
12. D2D Backup			✓
Sample Security Features:			
13. Secure Multi Tenancy			✓
14. Encryption at Rest	✓		
15. Encryption to Tape	✓		

How many possible combinations of selections are possible in this example? 45? 225?

Believe it or not, in this table alone, there are over **14 million** possible combinations. That's based on just 15 selections, each with only 3 configuration choices!

> **Doing the Math:** For any math majors out there, the exact number of possible combinations for the above table example is 14,348,907, or 3^{15} (that's three to the fifteenth power)!

Now, let's broaden our limited example for today's storage systems. Instead of just 15 features with three configuration options each, a modern storage system actually has dozens of tunable parameters, each with dozens of possible settings.

With so many tunable variables, there can also be any number of potential, negative consequences stemming from an improperly-tuned storage system.

This is why storage controller internal communication is so important today for highly efficient storage management. With a controller-based policy engine in place, the storage controller can calculate optimal configuration profiles to:

- Automatically enable the appropriate functionality
- Automatically map data to the most appropriate storage resources
- Automatically monitor resources and alert administrators of any out-of-policy conditions

With this advanced intelligence, human administrators are no longer tasked with trying to figure out how to configure storage for various users and applications. In the words of that great Pitchman Ron Popeil, when they install a new storage system, they should be able to just "set it and forget it."

The Future: Trends and Predictions

In terms of the external storage nervous system, having two major camps of storage (block-based and file-based) and five protocols for delivering this data has become a very inefficient model, indeed.

Buying different storage systems to accommodate different needs is quickly becoming passé. Data growth is unpredictable. Just as DAS environments were inflexible and unable to share storage resources, disparate SAN and NAS systems that can't share capacity have also become unacceptable.

The first step toward eliminating the need for disparate storage systems has already occurred: Unified storage. In fact, today, storage systems that do not support both block-based and file-based standards and all five protocols discussed earlier in this chapter are considered unsuitable for enterprise use.

The real question that remains is, "Will we ever arrive at a single, monolithic storage architecture?"

Although we alluded to Object Storage as a possible replacement for all protocols, unfortunately, history tells us that the continual innovation in storage communications requires that new standards and new ways of communicating across the enterprise won't allow us to get comfortable with any communication standard for very long.

Whether the next breakthrough in storage protocols and communication becomes object-based storage, SONET, RDMA (or some other protocol none of us has heard of yet), storage systems will be required to support these standards *in addition to* -- not instead of -- the existing standards.

Endnotes Referenced in Chapter 7

68 http://www.sdsc.edu/supercomputing/gordon/.
69 http://www.ecnmag.com/news/2013/03/superhero- supercomputer-helps-battle-autism.
70 http://www.ehow.com/about_4569555_the-nervous-system.html.
71 http://en.wikipedia.org/wiki/Storage_Module_Device.
72 http://en.wikipedia.org/wiki/ST-506.
73 http://en.wikipedia.org/wiki/Enhanced_Small_Disk_Interface.
74 http://www.snia.org/education/dictionary/c/#common_internet_file_system.
75 www.snia.org/education/dictionary/i/#internet_small_computer_systems_interface
76 http://en.wikipedia.org/wiki/Arbitrated_loop
77 http://www.webopedia.com/TERM/P/packet_collision.html.
78 http://files.shareholder.com/downloads/EXTR/2513956232x0x614179/bbdf0b9f-93f9-411b-adfd-5603462fd0b9/EXTR_News_2012_11_13_General.pdf.
79 http://www.storagenewsletter.com/news/connection/brocade-6520-switch.
80 http://ntsblog.burtongroup.com/network_and_telecom_strat/2009/03/data-center-ethernet-dce-the-one-wire-solution-1-of-3.html.
81 http://www.cisco.com/en/US/solutions/ns340/ns517/ns224/ns945/unified_fabric.html.
82 http://www.netapp.com/us/products/platform-os/data-ontap-8/unified-architecture.aspx.

Chapter Eight: It's The Efficiency, Stupid.

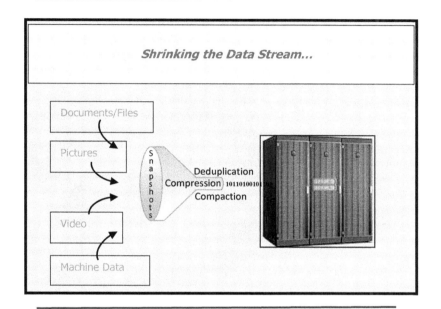

As depicted above, today's enterprise storage systems combine a variety of efficiency techniques to reduce the physical capacity needed to store data. Techniques like compression, deduplication and compaction can substantially reduce storage capacity requirements.

* * *

Something Happened on the Way to Efficiency

The title for this chapter is taken from James Carville's famous advice to Bill Clinton during the 1992 presidential campaign: "It's the economy, stupid."[83]

Carville's advice stemmed from the fact that Clinton's opponent was touting success in foreign diplomacy and the end to the cold war, but what American voters *really* wanted was a better economy. The strategy worked.

Storage efficiency forms an interesting parallel. While storage vendors tout flash-based SSDs and software-defined storage, users are being swamped by unprecedented data growth. Fundamentally, what users want is *more efficient* storage.

Considering that a typical enterprise IT budget is several million dollars per year, and data storage equipment consumes about a quarter of each IT dollar, its little wonder that these organizations are crying uncle![84]

What is storage efficiency? I'll define it simply here:

Storage efficiency allows smaller and smarter storage systems to do the work formerly performed by larger storage systems.

In this chapter we'll be discussing the evolution of storage efficiency within the storage industry.

The Past: Imposed Efficiency

In the early days of computing, efficiency was a necessity. I'll offer an example of what I mean from my own days as a young system engineer back in the '80s.

One of my customers back then was a large defense contractor on the East Coast. Their data center consisted of a huge IBM 370/168, water-cooled, mainframe computer with several dozen washing machine-sized 300MB disk drives attached. State-of-the-art for its time, the total storage capacity was 9.6 GB.[85]

> **Then & Now:** While 9.6GB seemed like a lot of storage back then, your teenager would not be so impressed. It now represents just slightly more capacity than a first-generation iPod.

Despite what seemed like a large disk storage capacity for that time, I also remember this data center being crammed with row upon row of reel-to-reel tape racks, similar to what's shown in Figure 8-1.

Figure 8-1. Information Stored on Reel-to-Reel Tape Racks.

The sparse density and high cost of storage in those days meant you couldn't have all your data handily available on disk. This necessitated efficiency. In effect, you had to run a litmus test to determine which data could remain on the available disk storage.

> **Imposed Efficiency in Action:** If a particular piece of data wasn't being used by the computer, it wasn't allowed to stay on disk. It was either spooled off to tape or just deleted (if it was already on tape). At the time, data on disk was viewed as an extension of system memory which offered space for work currently being processed.

As application data grew, and more users needed access to more data, of course, keeping data on disk became more and more important. This led to the concept of "data warehousing," originally promoted by IBM researchers Paul Murphy and Barry Devlin.[86]

As recently as 1996, companies with (gasp!) a terabyte of data warehoused on disk were considered so cutting-edge that a Terabyte Club was formed for these data consumers.

> **The Terabyte Club: An Elite Society of Users.** Formed in June 1996 as a special interest group by the Data Warehousing Institute, the Terabyte Club had a tough time getting off the ground. Why? So few companies back then had terabyte-sized databases.[87] (Today, of course, you can walk into any computer retailer and walk out with a 1TB disk drive under your arm for well under a hundred dollars.)

Storage Becomes Cheap to Buy, but Costly to Manage

So what happened between the time of monstrous 1TB corporate data warehouses and the present day, where 1TB disk drives are used to store the TV shows in your DVR?

I'll tell you what happened: Disk drives got much smaller, capacities got much bigger, and as a result, storage got very cheap.

Figure 8-2. The Incredible Shrinking Disk (Over Three Decades).[88]

And, what was the human response? To buy disk drives in droves. Enterprise data centers became filled with thousands of little disk drives with their relentless blinking lights. The '90s became the era of cheap disk.

> **How Much is that Disk Drive in the Window?** In 1990,
> you could buy a 320MB disk drive for roughly a thousand
> dollars. A decade later, in 2000, that same thousand-dollar
> investment would now buy you a 4GB drive, a 10X capacity
> boost. In 2016, you could buy a 10TB disk drive for far less
> than a thousand dollars and receive roughly 30,000 times
> greater capacity than that original 320MB disk from two
> decades ago.

Throughout the 1990s and 2000s, disk capacity grew almost as fast as the stock market in the booming dot-com; pre-recession days. But, unlike the market, disk drive capacities never saw their bubbles burst!

After the first compact (1GB) disk drives became available circa 1990, disk drive vendors soared faster than you could say, "Moore's Law." Disk drive capacities also soared exponentially, as shown in Figure 8-3.

Figure 8-3. Exponential Growth in Disk Drive Capacities.[89]

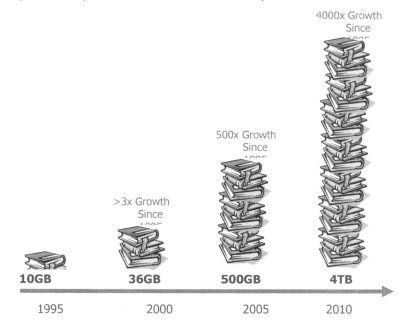

10GB	36GB	500GB	4TB
1995	2000	2005	2010

The Hard Truth: Cheap Disk Didn't Equal Cheap Storage

Disk capacities continued to grow and prices continued to drop. At the same time, data consumption was running amok. System administrators went crazy just trying to keep up with the demand.

They were soon racking up shelf after shelf of DAS, SAN, and NAS storage as fast as possible.

At some point, someone finally stopped and said, "Hey, how are we supposed to manage all this data?"

While it's true that disk had become cheap, the management of the data had become very expensive, indeed!

During this era we learned that cheap disk does not equal cheap storage.[90] Things began to spiral out of control.

Efforts were needed, on the part of both software vendors and storage system vendors, themselves, to make the management of storage easier and more efficient. The next sections cover two areas that developed with that aim:

- The emergence of SRMs to help manage ever-growing volumes of storage
- The emergence of storage efficiency to effectively store more data in less space

SRMs: Making Storage Easier to Manage

The fast growth of data coupled with lack of management led to the emergence of a large group of storage resource management (SRM) software vendors in the late '90s.

Companies with funny names like Creekpath, Astrum, Datacore, Storability (and a few dozen others) opened their doors and began to offer a better way to manage all of the data that was accumulating so rapidly.

What occurred with these companies was a very unusual phenomenon in our industry. Like the preponderance of early disk drive vendors who quickly appeared then vanished, the SRM vendors also began to pop up and disappear. In the case of SRM vendors, however, they were disappearing for a completely different reason.

SRM software had become so highly sought after by customers that the major storage players realized they were missing out on a significant opportunity. Their answer? They began to scoop up the SRMs!

This is best illustrated by Table 8-1 which demonstrates the outcome of 25 startup companies who offered SRM products in 2000. Of these, you'll notice:

- 19 were acquired by larger companies
- Two went belly-up
- Four still exist today as independent SRM providers

Table 8-1. The Fate of Early SRM Vendors.

SRM Vendors: Where Are They Now?		
Company	SRM Product	Current Status
AppIQ	AppIQ Manager	Acquired by HP in 2005
Arkivio, Inc.	Auto-Stor	Acquired by Rocket Software in 2008
Astrum Software	Astrum 1.5	Acquired by EMC in 2003
CreekPath Systems	CreekPath AIM Suite	Acquired by Opsware in 2006
Datacore	SANsymphony 5.0	Still independent

SRM Vendors: Where Are They Now?		
Company	SRM Product	Current Status
Software		
FalconStor Software	IPStor	Still independent
InterSAN	Pathline	Acquired by Finisar in 2005
Intermine	FileCensus	Still independent
Invio Software	Storage Practice Manager	Acquired by VERITAS in 2005
MonoSphere	Storage Manager	Acquired by Quest Software in 2009
NTP Software	Storage Reporter	Acquired by VERITAS in 2002
Netreon	SANexec Manager	Acquired by Computer Associates in 2003
Northern Parklife	Quota Server	Still independent
NuView	StorageX	Acquired by Brocade in 2006
Onaro	SANscreen	Acquired by NetApp in 2007
PowerQuest	PowerExpert SRM	Acquired by Symantec in 2003
Precise Software	StorageCentral SRM	Acquired by VERITAS in 2003
Prisa Networks	VisualSAN	Acquired by EMC in 2002
ProvisionSoft	DynamicIT	Acquired by Storability in 2003
Storability	Global Storage Manager	Acquired by StorageTek in 2004
Storage Networks	STORos Storage Manager	Ceased operations in 2003
Tek-Tools	Storage Profiler	Acquired by SolarWinds 2010
TeraCloud	SpaceNet	Became Estorian, acquired by 21st Century Software in 2012
Trellisoft	StorageAlert	Acquired by IBM/Tivoli 2002
TrueSAN Networks	Cloudbreak	Ceased operation in 2003

What Was So Great About SRM?

As you can see in Table 8-1, the SRM market was clearly onto something! Storage resource management software had begun to help manage the data growth explosion of the late '90s and early 2000s.

To understand more about the benefits of SRM software, the following definition offers a good start:

"Storage resource management (SRM) involves one or more techniques or software processes that can help optimize the efficiency, speed and overall utilization of available disk drive space (or capacity) in a storage array, like the capacity associated with a storage area network (SAN) or network-attached storage (NAS) system. In recent years, numerous SRM software programs have become available that help storage administrators perform SRM functions that would otherwise require time-consuming manual effort.

"Functions of an SRM program are varied and may include data storage, data collection, data backup, data recovery, SAN performance analysis, storage virtualization, storage provisioning, forecasting of future needs, maintenance of activity logs, user authentication, protection from hackers and worms, and management of network expansion. An SRM solution may be offered as a stand-alone software product, as part of an integrated program suite or as a built-in software component of an overall storage hardware system."[91]

SRM software was a welcome addition to the evolution of storage intelligence and made it easier for organizations to manage their growing volumes of data. Using SRM functionality, administrators could now more easily answer questions, such as:

- Which storage systems are under performing?
- Which storage systems are over performing?
- How do you balance your data so that all storage systems are performing at the optimal level?

While SRM functionality proved useful at helping to solve some of these issues, there remained, however, a few areas where it continued to fall short. In particular, these areas included:

- Capacity utilization
- Capacity optimization

Ultimately, these two areas were better left to the storage system itself. This was largely due to the fact that SRM products have a server-side view of the storage array. To a large extent, this prevents them from knowing the inner workings of the storage controller and its specific storage virtualization techniques.

Storage Becomes More Efficient and Easier to Manage

Despite the progress of early SRM solutions toward easier storage management, the two remaining areas (capacity utilization and capacity optimization) required software advances within the storage systems themselves.

In effect, it required a concerted move to develop more efficient storage.

In the next few segments, we'll explain why storage capacity utilization became such an issue in the first place. We'll then offer a glimpse of the main capacity optimization features that evolved to efficiently address these challenges.

The Capacity Illusion: What You See is Not Always What You Get

To understand about capacity utilization, it might help to first learn more about system reserves. Here's a brief explanation. . .

One of the key functions of a good SRM product is capacity reporting. Most people know that when they buy a 25TB storage system from their friendly storage vendor to support that new database, their "usable" capacity is going to be less than the 25TB. In some cases, it may be much less.

What we are talking about here is "system reserves." System Reserves typically consist of things like hot spare drives, parity drives, operating system overhead and a few other vendor-dependent features that steal your available storage capacity.

All storage vendors need some reserves, although they will vary slightly according to each vendor's architecture. As an example, Figure 8-4 shows the capacity profile and system reserves of a NetApp storage system.

Figure 8-4. Example of Capacity Available vs. Unavailable for Use.

Data ONTAP Capacity Allocation

Raw Capacity	System Reserve Capacity	Fixed Reserve Capacity	Kernel Overhead	Unavailable to Applications and Users
			RAID Checksum	
			WAFL Reserve	
			FlexVol Metadata	
		RAID Reserve/ Spare Drive Capacity	Hot Spare	
			Parity	
			Mirrored	
	Usable Capacity	Unused Reserve Capacity	Aggregate Snapshot Reserve	Potentially Available to Applications and Users
			Volume Snapshot Reserve	
			Volume Fractional Reserve	
			Vol/LUN/File Guaranteed Space	
		Available Capacity	Free Capacity	
			LUNs	Used Capacity
			Files	
			qtrees	
			Snapshots	
			Clones	
			SnapMirrors	
			SnapVaults	

If you compare the "Raw Capacity" bracket on the left of the diagram to the "Used Capacity" bracket at the bottom-right, it becomes fairly obvious that you are losing substantial capacity due to the amount taken for system reserves.

Ahoy! Underutilized Storage Ahead!

But that's not all. The "Used Capacity" shown in Figure 8-4 is probably not all that well-used. The common storage provisioning process followed by most IT organizations shows why this problem occurs:

- A storage administrator receives a provisioning request to accommodate the data storage needs of a new application.
- For most applications, it's often difficult for the administrator to predict the application's future data growth needs.
- In order to avoid either potential application disruptions down the road or any last-minute, urgent requests for added disk space, the administrator will typically overestimate the capacity needed for the application.
- The storage administrator then provisions traditional storage volumes and LUNs for the application based on this overestimated amount.

When traditional volumes and LUNs are provisioned in this way for specific applications, the space "carved out" of the storage system is initially void of any actual data. That provisioned disk space then only becomes utilized *after* the application has started to write data to disk.

Figure 8-5 shows the gap which can then develop between disk space available (i.e., "Available Capacity") and disk space actually used by the application (i.e., "Used Capacity"). This gap is where the underutilization problem occurs.

Figure 8-5. Space Available vs. Space Utilized Create a Utilization "Gap".

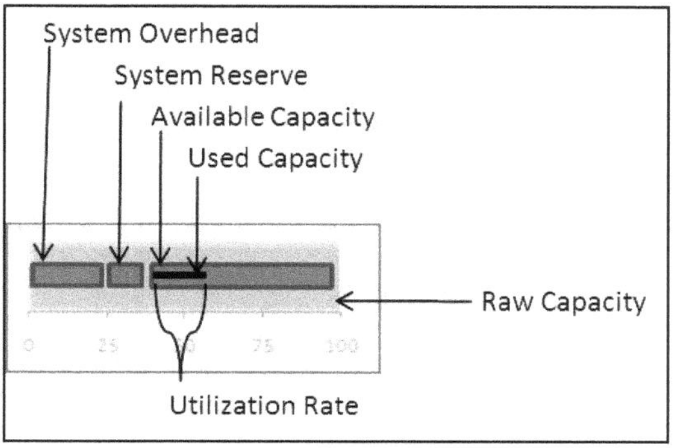

As a result of this utilization gap, only a fraction of the storage system capacity actually ends up containing written data. The result? That 25TB system you paid good money for might actually only be storing about 5TB of useful data!

Unfortunately, this is how storage has been provisioned for the past couple of decades: Lots of capacity, but very low utilization rates due to both system reserves and over-provisioned volumes and LUNs. In the past, most experts agreed that the typical enterprise data center operated at somewhere in the vicinity of 20% storage utilization.

Fortunately, present day storage systems have since evolved. They now offer several interesting new ways to raise utilization rates to much higher levels. Such methods vastly improve the efficiency of stored data.

Capacity Optimization: The Four Amigos

Why should you tolerate anything in the data center running at 20% efficiency? In my opinion, you shouldn't!

Today's storage vendors had the same opinion and have developed a set of features to help drive capacity optimization (i.e., storage efficiency) up to 100% and, even, beyond.

Believe it or not, there is a way to run a storage system at greater than 100% efficiency...if you know the tricks!

Let's start with the four capacity optimization features in wide use today:

1. Snapshots
2. Data deduplication
3. Data compression
4. Data compaction

It might be fair to think of these as "storage efficiency" features. Table 8-2 describes each in more detail.

These efficiencies are all available today and are rapidly gaining in popularity as users strive to increase storage utilization rates. You might be surprised to learn that these techniques can extend your storage system so that it easily stores 2-3 times more data than a traditional (inefficient) system. And most vendors don't charge anything for the addition of these features!

Table 8-2. Overview of Storage Efficiency Features.

Efficiency Feature	Description
1. Snapshots	Snapshots come in two flavors: Read-only and Writeable. Efficient read-only snapshots do not require any disk space when they are created, except for a small amount of metadata used in creating a second set of data pointers to the "live" data.
	Writeable snapshots also have an added benefit: You can use them to create clone copies of files, volumes, or LUNs. Although this concept is relatively new and users are still developing use cases, one obvious use of writeable snapshots is to use them when creating virtual machines (VMs) with the least

Efficiency Feature	Description
	amount of storage space required.
2. Data Deduplication	Data deduplication can either be done before the data is stored (referred to as inline deduplication) or after the data has been stored (referred to as post-process deduplication). In the case of disk-to-disk backup, dedupe can either be performed at the client (source) or at the backup appliance (destination). Regardless of the implementation, deduplication reduces the amount of physical disk capacity needed to store the data. It does this by removing redundant data and replacing it with reference pointers to the identical data already being stored.
3. Data Compression	Data compression has been around, well, since there was data. Lossless compression algorithms such as NRZ, L-Z and Gzip are very well understood. The thing that has prevented compression from creeping into storage arrays was that they required quite a bit of CPU horsepower. However, with the advent of faster multicore CPUs and more efficient software coding, disk data compression is now offered by several storage vendors today.
4. Data Compaction	Although it sounds a lot like data compression, data compaction uses a wholly different technique. Think of it as a suitcase-packing, trunk-packing, knapsack-packing type of solution. Most storage systems store data in fixed-size chunks However, due to fragmentation and padding, much of the data stored is smaller than these chunks. Like a high-speed game of Tetris, data compaction combines two or more of those small I/Os into one chunk before putting them down on the storage media.

The Future of Storage Efficiency

The quest for greater storage efficiency, however, doesn't end with just our four amigos mentioned earlier. Storage efficiency will continue to evolve.

In spite of storage devices with higher capacites and cheaper prices, the lesson we've learned from the past remains true today: Data will grow faster than the devices that store them. Just the same, it behooves users and the makers of storage systems themselves to keep systems ever more efficient and more easily manageable. (After all, storage management complexity is ultimately the real cost of enterprise storage.)

So, what does the future hold for storage efficiency? In the near future, high-performance Fibre Channel/SAS drives will likely become unnecessary. These will be replaced by multi-terabyte SATA drives with flash-based, front-end cache. In this scenario, front-end cache is likely to reside on both the drive and on the storage controller itself. This SATA/flash combination will be able to effectively eliminate the need for rows and rows of high speed (but low capacity) devices. It should also go a long way toward reducing the physical footprint of storage in the data center.

What else is in store? Storage systems will continue to pack more data per rack. In the current decade, they will also easily surpass petabytes of storage capacity per data center floor tile.

As with any evolution, such explosion of data introduces other IT management challenges: Tracking exactly what's stored where, let alone getting quick access to it.

Efforts to resolve this issue point toward the use of object storage, explained in the next section.

That Object (Storage) in your Mirror is Closer Than It Appears

To efficiently store and retrieve colossal amounts of data, the next generation of storage efficiency will most likely involve *object storage*. The reason object storage will become increasingly important is due to the fact that the majority of data growth in the past decade has come from *unstructured data* files. This trend will only proliferate.

Since we've just introduced a couple of new terms here, let's take a moment to describe each one. We'll start first with a useful definition of object storage that explains how this approach makes data easier to track.

Object Storage, Defined. . .

Object storage, also called object-based storage, is a generic term that describes an approach to addressing and manipulating discrete units of storage called objects.

Like files, objects contain data -- but unlike files, objects are not organized in a hierarchy. Every object exists at the same level in a flat address space called a storage pool and one object cannot be placed inside another object.

Both files and objects have metadata associated with the data they contain, but objects are characterized by their extended metadata. Each object is assigned a unique identifier which allows a server or end user to retrieve the object without needing to know the physical location of the data. This approach is useful for automating and streamlining data storage in cloud computing environments.

Object storage is often compared to valet parking at an upscale restaurant. When a customer uses valet parking, he exchanges his car keys for a receipt. The customer does not know where his car will be parked or how many times an attendant might move the car while the customer is dining. In

> this analogy, a storage object's unique identifier represents the customer's receipt.[92]

Because of the sheer volume of incoming data, it will soon become nearly impossible for IT to organize everyone's files in order to quickly and easily retrieve them. Therefore, expect to see more and more emphasis placed on object storage in the near future, for reasons described in the next section.

Now let's take a closer look at unstructured file data. The following definition should help.

> ### Unstructured Data, Defined. . .
>
> Unstructured data is a generic label for describing any corporate information that is not in a database. Unstructured data can be textual or non-textual. Textual unstructured data is generated in media like email messages, PowerPoint presentations, Word documents, collaboration software and instant messages. Non-textual unstructured data is generated in media like JPEG images, MP3 audio files and Flash video files.
>
> If left unmanaged, the sheer volume of unstructured data that's generated each year within an enterprise can be costly in terms of storage. Unmanaged data can also pose a liability if information cannot be located in the event of a compliance audit or lawsuit.[93]

Since the advent of email and office productivity files, the amount of unstructured data has risen dramatically. It's also predicted to keep growing rapidly. By some accounts, unstructured data accounts for 80% of all enterprise data and will grow 800% over the next five years.[94]

Something so large, growing so fast, is an indication of a big problem looming on the horizon.

As I was writing the book *Evolution of the Storage Brain* back in 2009, I came to this important realization:

> The problem before us is not the actual *storing* of data. It's *finding* the data you want, when you want it.

This need to find data—as opposed to just storing it—is why object storage will become so important. By encasing each object in a metadata 'wrapper,' you now bring structure to unstructured data. A logical hierarchy can be created that supports the efficient storage and retrieval of billions (or in Amazon's case, trillions![95]) of objects.

Endnotes Referenced in Chapter 8

83 http://en.wikipedia.org/wiki/It's_the_economy,_stupid.
84 http://idioms.thefreedictionary.com/Cry+Uncle.
85 http://en.wikipedia.org/wiki/IBM_System/370.
86 http://en.wikipedia.org/wiki/Data_warehouse.
87 http://www.informationweek.com/599/99mtter.htm..
88 http://royal.pingdom.com/2010/02/18/amazing-facts-and-figures-about-the-evolution-of-hard-disk-drives/.
89 http://www.pcworld.com/article/127105/article.htm.
90 http://devcentral.f5.com/weblogs/macvittie/archive/2009/10/07/disk-may-be-cheap-but-storage-is-not.aspx.
91 http://searchstorage.techtarget.com/sDefinition/0,,sid5_gci967890,00.html.
92 http://searchstorage.techtarget.com/definition/object-storage.
93 http://searchbusinessanalytics.techtarget.com/definition/unstructured-data.
94 http:/www.eweek.com/storage/slideshows/managing-massive-unstructured-data-troves-10-best-practices/.
95 http://aws.typepad.com/aws/2013/04/amazon-s3-two-trillion-objects-11-million-requests-second.html.

Chapter Nine: Storage In The Clouds

At times throughout this book, we've either disparaged mainframe computers or we've given them our admiration. This is a case where extra credit should be awarded. Mainframe computing brought forth the idea of "utility" computing. For decades, this idea has been well known. IBM, for instance, in the mid-80s, came up with the concept of "System-Managed Storage" that furthered the idea of drawing data from a utility pool of storage – in other words, cloud storage.

***

How the Human Brain Makes Us Smarter

The human brain follows an interesting path of logic. According to research conducted at the University of Oregon, although memory is important, it's not necessarily how much information people can "store" in their brains that dictates intelligence.

More, it relates to how successful they are at things like pattern-matching, identification, sorting and acting on what they deem the really important stuff inside their heads. Just as important, is the ability to filter out and ignore duplicate information already processed.[96]

I believe that data storage intelligence follows the same path. By its nature, one aspect of emerging storage system intelligence is the ability to help users automatically filter unnecessary data and allow them to efficiently retrieve the data that's most important to them.

Another aspect of data storage that parallels the logic of the human brain is the ability to "park" information based on its criticality. For example, if you start to put your hand on a hot stove, You'd better be able to instantly remember that this is a bad idea, whereas remembering Aunt Betty's phone number may not be quite so important and therefore can be stored in deeper recesses of the brain.

Fortunately, today's storage systems have the capability to instantly retrieve the most important information, while other less-important data can stored "deeper" to be accessed at a more leisurely pace.

This is where cloud computing (and cloud storage) comes into play. Most of us think of the cloud as some sort of vast repository of data in the sky, and in essence, that's just what it is. In an era of tremendous data growth, the cloud plays an important role in being an infinite "on-demand" repository of data that we don't necessarily need in an instant, but we may need someday.

In this chapter, we'll talk about the history of cloud computing, and the reasons it's become so important today (of course, also with a glimpse into the future).

The Past: Learning from the Mainframe

The mainframe epitomized centralized computing. All processing, business logic, applications, and data resided in the mainframe data center, what we used to call the *computer room*, in other words - the glass house.

When it comes to storage, the mainframe had one big advantage over today's client/server distributed computing model. Every byte of data stored on mainframe storage devices traveled through its central processing unit. This gives the mainframe the unique ability to monitor the placement of data and the utilization of storage devices.

In the early days, mainframe developers recognized this and proposed a "utility" computing model. Utility companies, they said, stored their energy resources in pipelines, reservoirs, and transmission lines which in turn were only provided to consumers as needed. Why, they reckoned, couldn't the same thing be done with mainframe computers and data storage?

John McCarthy was an early proponent of utility computing. Initially with BBN's time sharing system, and later during research at Stanford, he proselytized:

> *"If computers of the kind I have advocated become the*
> *computers of the future, then computing may someday be*
> *organized as a public utility just as the telephone system is a*
> *public utility... The computer utility could become the basis of*
> *a new and important industry.[97]"*

McCarthy didn't make his claim in the 2000s, the 1990s or even the 1980s. In fact, McCarty's statement came during a speech at MIT in **1961**! The computers he spoke of were not distributed, but rather, monolithic entities – sharing compute resources, networking, and data storage amongst many users.

Back in the day when computers were not easily afforded, the idea of time sharing, or utility, was a compelling way to spread the costs of computing (and storage) between many users – with the costs based on how much or how little they used. However, as costs dropped and inexpensive prepackaged software became available, the benefit of utility computing diminished and it eventually fell out of favor.

IBM never really abandoned the concept of the utility computing although the company apparently did stop talking publicly about it until the early years of this century. By 2003 IBM was talking about on-demand computing, which seemed remarkably like the utility concepts of the past.[98]

Here's how on-demand computing worked: you'd put a mainframe in your data center and pay for a certain amount of its system resource capacity, whether CPU, memory, or storage. Any time you needed more resources, you could request a key from IBM that would electronically unlock the additional resource capacity already embedded in the system. You paid for it on demand; only when you actually needed it.

On-demand computing would eliminate the common inefficiency of over-provisioning CPU, memory, and storage capacity, although that big mainframe was still taking up the same space, power, and cooling whether you used it all or not. This, however, was another attempt to use computing, and storage, as a utility, and pay for only what you used.

In the early 1990's HP, Unisys, and Computer Associates (CA Technologies today) started talking about a similar concept, although they used different marketing labels. To some it was utility computing, for others it was grid computing (as in the electric power grid). The systems were architected differently than IBM's, but the goal essentially was the same — to quickly and easily add system resource capacity when you needed it.

The Present: The Skies are Becoming Cloudy

Now, fast forward to the 2010s. Although the cost of computer hardware and software continued to drop, these reductions were being outpaced by rapidly growing requirements for more data, faster networks, and more powerful computers. As a result, there became a renewed interest in a utility-based IT model. Over-provisioning moved from an annoyance to a serious financial burden. During the Great Recession of 2007-2010, IT organizations could no longer afford the luxury of unrestrained spending in their quest to support necessary applications at unpredictable resource levels. They often needed to add system resources at any time and without much advance notice.

Cloud computing, with its promise of "just-in-time" IT resources, has emerged as the latest and perhaps final manifestation of time sharing, utility, on-demand, computing. Along the road to the cloud, there have been several twists and turns: Application Software Providers (ASPs), Managed Service Providers (MSPs), Storage Service Providers (SSPs), Software as a Service (SaaS) providers and many other market segments with equally confusing acronyms have been used to describe and deliver cloud-like services for several decades. "The cloud" has emerged as a general-purpose way of describing this evolution in computing.

> **Then & Now:** In the past, the "cloud" was commonly used in data center network diagrams to depict public and private external WAN networks. The cloud symbol in these network diagrams was understood to denote the demarcation point between that which was the responsibility of the network provider (usually a Telco) and that which was the responsibility of the IT organization.

Now, back to the mainframe and IBM. For several decades IBM has been exploring ways to do massive computing efficiently and reliably. These efforts tended to be based on either the mainframe, as was the case with Blue Gene, or a set of large Power Systems, as was the case with Watson.

This, however, is not the only way to go about this. Where IBM focused primarily on adopting its large scales systems, Amazon went the opposite way by connecting massive numbers of distributed servers (remember our discussion of Amazon's Dynamo model way back in Chapter 2)?

Today, Amazon's model has won out, and the world has become an interconnected web of servers and storage that emulate the functions a mainframe computer, but on a scale of enormity never before seen. Even IBM joined the fray in 2013 when it acquired SoftLayer for $2 Billion. SoftLayer's business model was described as follows[99]:

> *"SoftLayer lashes together bunches of servers and storage and rents them to its 23,000 corporate or government customers for use as their IT system so they don't have to own the equipment or manage it on premises...A lot of SoftLayer's customers are Web-native companies that can't afford lots of equipment but may suddenly, as in the case of a social game or new mobile app, need thousands of times the computing power they had predicted they'd need.*

The quote above describes SoftLayer (and the cloud) as a shared virtual infrastructure of servers, networks and storage in an on-demand configuration. If this sounds like utility computing, that's because it's exactly the same thing. Our industry has a habit of doing this—creating new names to describe things we've already invented.

> **Why do they call it the cloud, anyway?** The origin of the phrase **Cloud Computing** was inspired by Dr. Ramnath Chellappa, a professor at Emory University in a 1997 work titled *Intermediaries in Cloud-Computing*[100]. The paper was presented at the Dallas INFORMS conference in 1997. In the abstract, Dr. Chellappa writes:
>
> *"Computing has evolved from a mainframe-based structure to a network-based architecture. While many terms have appeared to describe these new forms, the advent of electronic commerce has led to the emergence of 'cloud computing.' This work aims at analyzing the role of agents and intermediaries enabling this framework.*

A Quick Flight Through The Cloud

So, why would anyone want to put their data into a cloud? Because it makes things easier for you. You don't really care what server your data lands on, or what storage system stores the data. You just know that your data is there, and can be easily accessed.

A commonly discussed aspect of cloud computing is the idea of public and private clouds. As the name implies, this has to do with who has access to the data in their cloud. Private clouds refer to data tucked away behind a corporate firewall with restricted (i.e. employees only) access, while a public cloud refers to storage that can be shared by many companies or people (also called "tenants").

Of course, our industry being what it is, we've come up with yet another type of cloud: The hybrid cloud. A hybrid cloud combines the attributes of both public and private clouds. In my earlier book I wrote that:

> "I can't imagine why anyone would actually set up a hybrid cloud instead of having separate public and private clouds..."

Well, as it turns out, the hybrid cloud is the one model that everyone is striving for today, for reasons we'll go into later in this chapter. But first, let's discuss some common characteristics of all clouds, whether private, public, or hybrid.

When You Think Cloud, Think S.A.V.E.

One way to think about the cloud is with the SAVE acronym:

- **S**ecure
- **A**utomated
- **V**irtual
- **E**fficient

Here's a little more detail about each part of this acronym:

- **Secure** – Clouds often share IT resources across multiple tenants. Therefore, it's imperative that secure multi-tenancy be in a cloud's design. This ensures there's no cross-pollination of data between users.

- **Automated** - Because shared cloud infrastructures can quickly grow by epic proportions, automation is a must. It should include automatic workflows that accommodate load balancing, data protection, and alerts for out-of-policy conditions.
- **Virtual** – Creating shared IT resources requires virtualization at all levels. What began as virtual servers has since been extended to virtualized storage and virtual networks.
- **Efficient** – The primary motivation for moving data to a cloud is to save time and money, or in other words, efficiency: a more efficient use of pooled IT resources and a more efficient process in provisioning such resources for users. For servers and storage, efficiency also means saving money by raising utilization rates and consolidating physical devices.

From a data storage perspective, the cloud begins with virtual storage pools. Drawing from the days of utility storage, let's investigate the fundamental properties of storage pools.

Virtual storage pools allow you to:

- Seamlessly add or remove storage systems from the pool.
- Automatically assign volumes and LUNs to the pool by using the policy that best defines the attributes you need for that volume or LUN.
- Transparently move data between storage systems in the pool as capacity or performance needs change.

The ultimate responsibility of virtual storage pools is this: Being able to more cleanly automate and share underlying storage resources in order to offer them in a relatively "on-demand" way to meet both peak and regular traffic loads across a variety of application environments.

The concept of virtual storage pools provides users with flexible, expandable storage arrays.

The Future of Cloud Computing: Fact and Fiction

The cloud model of virtual compute and virtual storage is predicted by many to become the darling of IT in the very near future. Leveraging the economics of cloud, organizations that would have normally required enormous amounts of capital will only need a fraction of what was previously required using the cloud's "pay-as-you-go" model.

Another factor driving cloud adoption is the centralization of shared data. An abundance of related data can be shared, allowing renewed insight through the centralization of huge databases (otherwise known as "big data"). With collaborative access to this type of data, patient healthcare improves, population trends are assimilated, and customer service is enhanced. Where else to store these vast databases, with global access, but in the cloud?

Finaly, an emerging view is that the biggest reward in cloud adoption will be *agility*. As business demands increase at ever faster rates, it's becoming clear that traditional IT approaches of purchasing and installing on-premise servers and storage won't meet this need. As such, organizations will look to the cloud for rapid deployment. Cost savings, while still important, will no longer the leading driver of a move to cloud.

Will these three benefits (cost savings, shared data, and increased agility) signal the end of IT-owned data centers? Not so fast, we say. For every point, there is a counterpoint, will these will be considered in the following paragraphs.

One popular theory is that everyone will save money by migrating applications and data to the cloud, but that's not always the case. The fact that most IT organizations leverage multiple cloud providers means enterprises are waist-deep in complex cloud vendor management, and the fact is that determining your actual cloud costs can be very difficult, as anyone who has ever tried to dissect their cable TV or mobile device monthly statements can attest. Also, if applications are particulary I/O intense, IT can actually spend more money than they did with on-premises solutions. In many publicized use cases, organizations have found that cloud costs to be in the millions of dollars, and reverted back to traditional data centers.

In regards to data collaboration, the unfortunate reality is the collaboration requires collaborators. Government privacy regulations, intellectual property concerns, and a general reluctance to share company data are all obstacles that need to be overcome.

The third point – agility – also has its detractors. Many organizations are discovering that their existing culture and processes are an impediment to using cloud to drive agility.

This phenomenum manifests itself in several ways. Old school IT organizations will struggle with their role in the cloud world – as they did during the transition from mainframe to client/server. Old habits are hard to die. These struggles will lead to adverse effects on jobs, roles and skills.

The cloud opens up new opportunities, but only for those willing to embrace this new world.

Oh, the Places We'll Go

In 2017, it is clear that the "great migration" to the cloud is set to take place, where we'll see more workloads moving to cloud-based platforms than ever before. We'll also have issues and problems, some that we are familiar with and some we have not seen before. In spite of this, cloud security and performance will continue to improve, as well as management.

Clouds have come a long way in the last ten years. Amazon built the prototype hyper-scale cloud provider model, and is expected to remain king of the clouds for the foreseeable future. Amazon has done a good job in reacting to the needs of their users, and focusing on the hard problems. Along with Amazon (AWS) - Microsoft (Azure), Google (GCP) and and IBM (SoftLayer) will remain the elite cloud providers.

But before you write them off, private data centers aren't going away. Although the balance of power within the cloud provider world won't change much, there will continue to be a need to keep data on-premises for cultural, legal, and privacy reasons. A great majority of enterprise organizations will straddle the line between data-center-based private clouds and the public cloud, embracing a hybrid cloud model.

Welcome to the Hotel California

To service these established organizations, public cloud companies will need to improve their hybrid cloud offering. A key feature will be cloud data portability, or the ability of move data between private cloud networks and public cloud providers, or from one public cloud provider to another. Up until now, the providers have been very protective of their user base, and have made it difficult to move data from their cloud (as the song goes - you can check in any time, but you can never leave...)

We've spent a lot of time in the clouds in this chapter, for good reason. Some have said that cloud computing and cloud-enabled storage will become the way we store our data for decades to come - at least some of our data.

With the help of modern storage network technology; fast, cheap Ethernet connections; and intelligent, efficient storage techniques—there may well be something in the clouds for us all. For inactive data, and for start-up companies building their initial IT infrastructure, the cloud is a no-brainer.

For established companies with decades of data center experience, however, the path to the cloud wil be slower. In another ten years, we'll predict that the majority of primary enterprise application data will still reside within the walls of corporations.

Endnotes Referenced in Chapter 9

96 http://techdirt.com/articles/20051129/188238_F.shtml.
97 https://en.wikipedia.org/wiki/Utility_computing
98 http://www.zdnet.com/article/ibm-on-demand-computing-has-arrived/
99 http://www.forbes.com/sites/bruceupbin/2013/06/04/ibm-buys-privately-held-softlayer-for-2-billion/#2d5111617d88
100 http://www.bus.emory.edu/ram/

***

Chapter Ten: The Era Of Scale

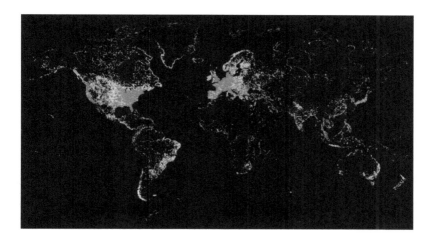

The above illustration depicts a typical internet heat map. A popular phrase these days is *The Internet of Things* (IoT), which refers to the internetworking of physical devices, vehicles, buildings, sensors, actuators, and the network connectivity that enable these objects to collect and exchange data. Many experts believe that the IoT will consist of over 50 billion objects by 2020.

* * *

A New Era in Storage

As I've maintained throughout this book, I firmly believe you're better prepared to grasp and act upon what's unfolding in storage today when you look back at what came before it.

Along this same vein, I've devoted this chapter to a key inflection point in the evolution of data storage: The emerging 4th era of scale out storage.

To better understand this new era requires seeing its emergence within the context and backdrop of the three main eras that defined data storage before it.

In this chapter, you'll learn about:

- Each of the three prior eras of data storage
- The triggers that signaled a shift from one era to the next
- The emergence of scale out storage at the start of the fourth era

We have a lot of ground to cover here, so join me and let's get started.

Scale Out in Context within the Eras of Data Storage

Up until now, the evolution of data storage was defined by three eras (as shown in Table 10-1). Within this context, scale out storage as ushering in the fourth era. In this segment, We'll see why.

Table 10-1. The Four Eras of Data Storage.

Era	From	Description
#1	1950s to early 1980s	**The Birth of Commercial Computing.** This first era of data storage was characterized by very large and expensive storage devices. In fact, old-timers still use the acronym, SLED (Single Large Expensive Disk) to describe these devices.
#2	Early 1980s to mid-1990s	**Data For One and All.** In the second era, inexpensive small form factor (SFF) disk drives became available. These led to experimentation and the eventual delivery of large storage arrays with dozens (or hundreds) of these small storage devices grouped together.
#3	Mid-1990s to early 2010s	**Optimizing For Speed and Efficiency.** In the third era, storage virtualization led to breakthroughs that provided an abstraction layer between the physical constraints of storage devices and the logical way in which they were presented to servers.
#4	Early 2010s and Beyond	**A Data-Driven Society.** This emerging fourth era is characterized by immense scale, public clouds, and scale out storage systems.

Clues Heralding the Transition to a New Era

Interestingly enough, a single theme drove each transition from era to era – the relentless creation of data; and an inflection point where lack of innovation threatened to become a limiting factor to business and society:

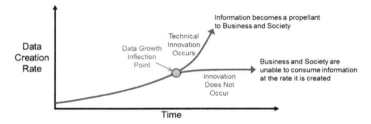

Today, data growth has again forced us to innovate as we transition into a fourth era in the evolution of modern data storage.

This fourth era will be characterized by immense scale and never-before- seen complexity.

In the next few sections, we'll briefly delve into each prior era. As we examine each era, you'll see why we are now on the cusp of another major data storage transition: This time to one of scale out storage.

Era #1: Commercial Computing is Born

Table 10-2 sums up a few of the key innovations that occurred in the first era of data storage.

Table 10-2. First Era: Innovations and Birth of Commercial Computing.

Year	Innovation
1952	**Mainframe Computing.** Early business computers such as the IBM 701[101] and those that followed paved the way for businesses to streamline costs and operations.
1957	**New Storage Devices.** Storage devices such as the IBM 305 RAMAC were created in order to house an ever-increasing amount of online data.
1960	**Business Applications.** GE's Integrated Data Store (IDS[102]) and IBM's Information Management System (IMS[103])—along with COBOL-based business applications—drove a complete retooling of business processes in the 1960s.

Before computers entered the office of the modern-day business, three critical office technologies were in place:

- The typewriter
- The adding machine
- A filing system

Financial number-crunching was done manually (invariably with a large margin of error).

Between the 1950s and 1960s, mainframe computers started to give the business world a new and exciting edge. Business operations could be done faster and more accurately than ever before. The business world could now operate at a much faster rate.

Time was the major advantage brought by computers.

The data collected by mainframe computers was stored first on punch cards. It was also printed on green bar paper.

Early data growth, however slight, soon made such rudimentary data collection methods impractical. Efforts to find better ways to store companies' growing volume of data would lead to the development of a new-fangled storage device: the disk drive.

Over time, commercially packaged applications from companies such as Cullinet and Computer Sciences Corporation gave birth to a burgeoning software industry that today is worth an estimated $300 billion[104].

The rapid proliferation of mainframe computers, and a parallel growth in applications meant that data creation was on a steep curve, too steep for early disk drives to keep pace with. Something new was needed…

Era #2: The Age of Discovery

New data storage technologies began to appear in the early 1980s. Table 10-3 lists a few of the key innovations that enabled the second era of data storage.

Table 10-3. Second Era: Innovations and the Age of Discovery.

Year	Innovation
1980	**Small Form Factor Hard Disk Drives (HDD).** The emergence of small, inexpensive, disk drives allowed for the formation of large storage arrays.
1986	**Small Computer Systems Interface (SCSI).** SCSI gave us the common framework to tie all those small drives together.
1987	**Redundant Array of Independent Disk (RAID).** RAID protected us against failures of inexpensive drives that might have otherwise brought down an entire storage system.

Year	Innovation	
1988	**Network-Attached Storage (NAS).**	Both NAS and SAN gave us the ability to cut the umbilical cord of storage, thereby creating infinitely expandable networks.
1990	**Storage Area Networks (SAN).**	

As we entered the 1980s, it became clear that data growth had become prolific. The second era in the evolution of storage was driven again by breakthroughs in storage device hardware.

First, SLEDs were replaced by inexpensive storage devices connected, en masse, into large storage systems via a common protocol language (SCSI). However, since these inexpensive devices were prone to failure, a mechanism was needed to allow them to operate regardless of failure. That mechanism was RAID.

Finally, a broad storage network (SAN and NAS) was needed for the storage systems to communicate quickly and easily with an alarming number of application servers that now seemed to be popping up everywhere.

Once these second era storage pieces were in place, the stage was set for even greater proliferation of data. The subsequent data explosion was a direct outcropping of this newly created world of interconnected clients and servers.

Now, instead of the data being consumed by only a privileged few, data was now being distributed across the entire business rank and file.

Business and society were just beginning to grasp the power that this new-found data held. Throughout the 1980s, new software giants emerged, companies such as Oracle, Adobe, and of course, Microsoft.

The end of data growth was nowhere in sight. People, it seemed just couldn't get enough data. This abundance of data was bringing the world into the exciting new information age. At the same time, it was creating misery amongst IT architects who were constantly trying to satisfy the hunger of people starving for more data. As we entered the 1990s, it was clear that we were on a collision course with yet another data growth inflection point.

Era #3: The Age of Optimization

This brings us to the current, third era of data storage: the age of optimization. This era was, again, a response to the steady growth of data. Table 10-4 shares a few of the key innovations that occurred in this era.

Table 10-4. Third Era: Innovations and the age of optimization.

Year	Innovation
1995	**Virtualized Storage Array.** The virtualized storage array taught us that storage need not be bound by physical disk properties.
2002	**Storage Resource Management (SRM).** SRM software brought stability to rapidly growing storage infrastructures.
2010	**Public Cloud.** TCP/IP internet connectivity allowed the public cloud to succeed in building a worldwide infrastructure of cheap storage at infinite scale. This feat was accomplished, in spite of the fact that earlier storage service providers (SSPs) had failed at the same task.

During this third era, storage systems became adept at processing data transactions at the speed of light.

To the storage system, more and larger device capacities meant simply that more data and more read/write requests that needed to be handled instantly.

Luckily, at the same time, faster controller CPUs with more memory meant processing power could be allocated to intelligence beyond that required just to service basic read/write requests. Such processing power could now also be used for storage *virtualization*.

Storage virtualization meant that a disk drive was no longer just a disk drive. Instead, a disk drive became a set of logically addressed blocks now able to be manipulated.

Storage resource management (SRM) evolved sending an alarm when something broke to now being part of a sophisticated control plane that could observe and proactively manage all storage systems from a single view.

Another key development occurred during the third era was the emergence of cloud providers who realized that Internet connectivity had reached a point where they could successfully store and move vast amounts of data, and move this data from point A to point B, even when either point was located anywhere in the world.

Welcome to Era #4: The Age of Massive Scale out

The innovations of each era, driven by data growth, caused a fundamental shift in how business could operate. Each era contained technologies that solved a particular data growth problem that otherwise would have brought data and business momentum to an inconvenient halt.

Desperation, as they say, is often a key motivational factor that drives innovation.

As this book is being written, on the horizon, yet another data growth inflection point is emerging, driven by, among other things, a wave of machine-generated data. Some predict that "the internet of things" will soon reach 1 Trillion devices, all generating data. Current data storage technologies simply cannot keep pace with such monumental data growth caused by our data-driven society and the insatiable thirst for even more data.

This fourth era of data storage, like the others before, will require new technologies and innovation. Foundational to the success of this era will be scale out capabilities, as described in Table 10-5.

Table 10-5. *4th Era - The era of massive scale: 2017-??.*

Year	Innovation
now	**Scale out Storage.** Massive pools of virtualized storage
soon	**Software-defined Storage.** Self-managed, automated storage
later	**Data Portability.** Hybrid clouds with the ability to move large amounts of data between clouds as needed
much later	**Data Harvesting.** Data becomes commodity that can be harvested, priced, and sold

Applying What We've Learned Thus Far

For many years the standard storage array had two controllers (for redundancy) and a lot of disk trays containing hundreds of disks (or SSDs). The controllers connected via storage area network (SAN) or network attached storage (NAS) and provided storage to their connected application servers. All of the disk trays were connected through the storage controllers and all application servers accessed these disks through the two controllers. To increase the capacity of the array, more shelves full of disks were added to the same controllers. For the past 20 years or so, we have referred to this as *scale up* storage.

Scale out storage is very different and far more sophisticated than scale up storage. Scale out is common with cloud solution providers and it works like this: A large number of storage nodes work together providing aggregated capacity and performance that cannot be obtained by a single large storage array on its own. Often, cloud providers build their storage from a large number of commodity x86 servers to produce huge and highly distributed storage networks (remember Amazon Dynamo from Chapter Two? Aha! Now you're getting it!)

Here's why scale out storage is so important - as the load on a traditional storage array increases — often driven by virtualization of servers — and more disks (or SSDs) are added, the two controllers themselves become a bottleneck as each begins to require more and more CPU to support the increase in I/O. Eventually, enough disks are added until the controllers and CPU hit their performance ceiling and simply can do no more.

Adding more and faster disks/SSDs behind an overloaded controller pair only places more load on the controllers. In these systems once the controllers are saturated there is little you can do, apart from buying an additional new array with its own pair of controllers and moving some of the workload (VMs) onto the new array. A difficult task indeed.

Rather than using custom controller platforms, new scale out storage systems often use a group of x86 servers to form a storage *cluster*. Each server (i.e. node) is loaded with disks and uses a network — usually Ethernet — to talk to the other servers in the storage array. The group of servers together forms a clustered storage array and provides storage volumes over a network, just like a traditional array.

Adding additional server nodes to the cluster not only adds more storage capacity, but also adds more network ports, more CPU and more RAM. Therefore, as the capacity of a scale out cluster increases, its performance does not degrade. Another benefit is that adding nodes is generally non-disruptive, so a system outage is never required to upgrade the cluster.

The design of the cluster software determines how many nodes the cluster can handle. Some scale out storage is limited to a few server nodes; while others work with dozens or hundreds of nodes. If the array architecture scales to hundreds of nodes then these systems are capable of Petabytes of capacity and millions of storage operations per second.

The Future of Data Storage Looks Bright, and Cloudy

Applying an accumulated knowledge base gained over the past 60 years (and mostly covered in this book), the storage systems of tomorrow will employ many advanced concepts we've covered in storage hardware, device protection, networking, memory utilization, storage efficiency and of course software-defined constructs.

We are seeing storage systems today that maintain enterprise-grade features but use inexpensive hardware to keep pace with data growth without breaking the budget. Whether in the clouds or in traditional data centers, just as modular storage arrays replaced expensive mainframe storage, scale out storage clusters are signaling the demise of proprietary storage systems.

Putting it all into Perspective

There you have it: A look back at my years witnessing the evolution of data storage. I hope you've found our walk through storage history interesting and my future vision somewhat thought-provoking.

Before we conclude, there is one remaining point that I'd like to offer, as food for thought.

Over the past 30 years, IT organizations have seen their data grow by leaps and bounds. Earlier in this book, Chapter 8 to be specific, I mentioned a large customer of mine on the east coast in 1980 had an IBM 360 mainframe that contained roughly 10GB of external storage. This was typical of mainframe data capacity for the time. In 2010, from my earlier book, I estimated that the average data center housed roughly 100TB of active production data – giving us a 10,000-times increase in data capacity from 1980 to 2010.

Doing some quick math, these numbers equate to an average annual growth rate of 35.94%. Now, I wouldn't necessarily define 36% annual growth as explosive, but many vendors enjoy stating this. Rather, it reflects steady growth as we've transformed from a society based on slide rules and paper records into a society highly dependent on algorithms and digital information storage.

Over the next few pages, we'll walk through the 35.94% annual storage growth—and how it affected IT organizations in both the past and the future.

Table 10-6 begins with a look first at past data growth, while Table 10-7 offers a startling glimpse into the future.

Table 10-6. Data Growth: 1980-2010.

Year	Storage Capacity (terabytes)
35.94% annual data growth rate. *Year 1980 starts at 10GB (.01 TB)*	
1981	0.014
1982	0.018
1983	0.025
1984	0.034
1985	0.046
1986	0.063
1987	0.086
1988	0.117
1989	0.159
1990	0.216
1991	0.293
1992	0.398
1993	0.541
1994	0.736
1995	1.000
1996	1.360
1997	1.85
1998	2.51
1999	3.42
2000	4.64
2001	6.31
2002	8.58
2003	11.67
2004	15.86
2005	21.56
2006	29.31
2007	39.85
2008	54.17
2009	73.63
2010	100.15

Taking this a bit further, let's project the same growth rate for another 30 years. Notice that in 2017, the year this book is being published, the average amount of data stored by IT organizations in Table 10-7 is predicted to be 858TB. Based on discussions with numerous customers, that number is a realistic one, further validating the steady, constant, growth in data.

As with any exponential growth curve, as you move to the right of the curve, the results start to grow very fast, and our table is no exception.

Table 10-7. Data Growth: 2010-2040.

Year	Storage Capacity (terabytes)
35.94% annual data growth rate.	
2011	136
2012	185
2013	251
2014	341
2015	464
2016	631
2017	858
2018	1,166
2019	1,585
2020	2,155
2021	2,930
2022	3,983
2023	5,414
2024	7,360
2025	10,005
2026	13,601
2027	18,489
2028	25,133
2029	34,166
2030	46,446
2031	63,138
2032	85,830
2033	116.677
2034	158,611
2035	215,616
2036	293,109
2037	398,452
2038	541,656
2039	736,327
2040	1,000,963

As shown, that 35.97% growth rate applied over a 60-year period produces an astonishing *one million terabytes* (i.e. one Exabyte) of data to manage in the average data center in 2040! Will it actually be possible for a single organization to manage one Exabyte of data by 2040? How soon after that will we be discussing Zettabytes and Yottabytes with a straight face?

Looking back, I am sure if I tried to convince anyone in that 1980 data center that they might someday be responsible for managing 858TB, they would have revoked my access badge. After all, this is greater than 85,000 times more storage than they were used to seeing. But, here we are in 2017 and an Exabyte of data is becoming closer to reality. Things are going to be very interesting in the coming years...

Endnotes Referenced in Chapter 10

---

[101] https://en.wikipedia.org/wiki/IBM_700/7000_series
[102] http://www.computerworld.com/article/2588199/business-intelligence/the-story-so-far.html
[103] https://en.wikipedia.org/wiki/IBM_Information_Management_System
[104] https://en.wikipedia.org/wiki/Software_industry

***

Epilogue: Deceit, Theft, Espionage, and Murder

A few years ago, I took a break from my traditional technical blogging. Instead, I decided to relay a few stories from my data storage days of yore over the past 30+ years in the business. I dubbed this series, "Deceit, Theft, Espionage and Murder in the Storage Industry." If you think storage is boring or just want a break from the typical chatter, read on as I recount a few wicked plots that have been an infamous part of our industry.

* * *

Part 1: Deceit, Lost Earnings and a Shipment of Bricks

Woody Allen once said that most of what you get from life you get by just showing up. Well I've been showing up at work for over 30 years now and I've seen some pretty fascinating things happen during that time.

I know it's hard to believe, but long ago there were companies other than Seagate, Western Digital, and Hitachi that made disk drives.

Maxtor, Quantum, Micropolis, NEC, Control Data (later Imprimis) and IBM were some of the better known; while Rodime, PraireTek, and MicroScience were some of the lessor known.

Competition was fierce and capacities were growing faster than Arnold Schwarzenegger's biceps. This story focuses on a company called MiniScribe. MiniScribe was a disk drive company based in Longmont, Colorado who competed for its share of disk drive sales. In fact, MiniScribe was flying high in the midst of the desktop PC explosion in the mid-80's. But things started to sour for MiniScribe.

MiniScribe had become obsessed with growth that was fueled by lead investor and CMO (Chief Maniacal Officer) Q.T. Wiles. After 11 consecutive quarters of exceptional growth, MiniScribe lost a large contract with IBM, while simultaneously losing pending deals with Apple and DEC.

Desperation and panic ensued. Fake orders were created, broken drives were shipped, and companies that ordered 100 drives from MiniScribe found 500 on their loading dock. But that wasn't enough. In one of the most bizarre decisions ever made, MiniScribe execs decided to ship *bricks* to customers (in those days bricks were actually worth less than disk drives) with strict instructions that these boxes were not to be opened.

Unfortunately, MiniScribe was also laying off employees (Oops!), some of which were in on the scheme.

The result? A few phone calls later the scam was exposed in front page news on the Denver Post. MiniScribe was busted and quickly became an industry afterthought. I seem to recall that the term "shipping bricks" existed before this scandal, but MiniScribe certainly placed their indelible mark on the phrase.

Interestingly, no jail time was served in the MiniScribe case. Investors, auditors and other participants were fined in excess of $500 Million. Q.T. Wiles, who many believed was the main perpetrator, sank into obscurity. I suspect we'd see more severe punishment these days (i.e. "Back to your cell, Mr. Wiles, your hour in the recreation yard is over.")

There you have it. A major corporate scandal and we can claim it as part of our legacy! And you thought disk drives were boring...

Part 2: The Case of the Purloined Disk Drives

Back in the early 1990s, a couple of pals and I started a company to provide data storage for the exploding Sun Microsystems workstation market.

Our business plan (yeah, like we had one of those!) was to quickly scoop up the latest and greatest technology, slap it into a desktop chassis, and beat our competitors to the punch.

The data storage industry was undergoing its own space race, with vendors rolling out a steady supply of bigger, faster disk drives. The flavor of this day was Maxtor's 525MB drive. Maxtor had beat everyone else to the magic 500MB level, and these drives were hot commodities. Hotter, in fact, then I realized.

Part of my job at this company was procurement officer. Translation: I would buy the weekly edition of Computer Shopper at the local newsstand and scour the ads looking for folks offering the latest drives.

I spotted an ad for the treasured Maxtor drive and placed a quick call. "Sure, we have those drives. How many do you want?" they asked. I soon placed an order for about 100 of them. As I hung up, I thought to myself how odd it was that this seller offered such a cheap price for the drives. Attributing this to my shrewd negotiating skills, however, I went about my business.

A few days later, on a Friday as I recall, the drives showed up as promised and I began assembling them without too much further thought.

Talk about a Hot Disk Drive

The following Monday morning was bright and sunny, a beautiful day in the Boston Metro area. I saw another car in the lot as I pulled in to work but didn't think too much of it. I did notice, however, that two men in suits followed me to the front door. As I reached for my keys, one of them identified himself as an FBI agent and the other as a representative of Maxtor. Had I recently purchased some 525MB disk drives from Mr. X? I gulped and said, "Yes, I did."

They said they wanted to talk to me. This is where the story unfolded. Turns out Mr. X was part of a theft ring. Employees of Sun had been pocketing these nifty drives and emptying their pockets in his shop. Sun had noticed some accounting irregularities and began tracking serial numbers. The FBI wanted to take my drives and see if the serial numbers matched. Was I willing to cooperate?

Just then my partners arrived, and they looked at me like I was going to single-handedly bring the company down. Wouldn't you know it, the phone rang at that moment and it was Mr. X, asking if I got the drives OK. "Tell him you want to buy more drives," the FBI agent whispered as I feigned calmness talking to Mr. X. My head was spinning. Would I cooperate? Damn right I would!

Things calmed down a bit as the FBI agent loaded the drives into his trunk and thanked me for my cooperation. The fellow from Maxtor said they would replace all the drives with brand new ones and also thanked us for our help in sending Mr. X up the river, apparently they had been trying to nab this guy for quite a while and now finally had the evidence they needed.

Part 3: Espionage and Plug-in Storage

For this story, we go all the way back to 1972, when mainframes roamed the earth. In those days, the entire computer industry consisted of six companies: IBM and the BUNCH (Burroughs, Univac, NCR, Control Data and Honeywell.)

These companies hovered over their customers like protective parents, effectively blocking out their competitors with highly proprietary hardware and software.

Enter a little Tulsa-based company called Telex. Previously called Midwestern Instruments, Telex emerged from the oil and gas seismic industry with a clever device used for geophysical logging. This device was called the M-3000. The M-3000 was an analog magnetic recorder (or, in today's parlance: a tape drive).

Watching the emerging success of IBM's mainframe, the folks at Telex thought, "Hey, that new-fangled IBM computer uses tape drives, and we make tape drives!" The result was the first plug-compatible peripheral in history.

Telex had designed an IBM interface and channel controller that would plug directly into any IBM 360. And to the chagrin of IBM, the darn thing worked and Telex sold it much cheaper than the IBM model.

Not taking this lying down, IBM decided to try and persuade potential Telex buyers not to associate themselves with this upstart company, to the point where they would refuse to service the entire computer if anyone dared attach a foreign device to their precious mainframe.

Suits, Countersuits and a Stalemate

As a result, Telex was losing sales and in trouble. Having little choice, Telex sued IBM on January 21, 1972. Telex complained that IBM violated antitrust laws and used predatory practices designed to force Telex out of business.

The case trudged through the courts. In December of 1973, a district court finally ruled in favor of Telex and awarded them $352 Million. IBM quickly appealed the decision and launched a counter-suit, alleging that Telex engaged in industrial espionage. How else, they reckoned, was Telex able to figure out how to connect their alien device to our mother ship?

IBM claimed that ". . .Telex had engaged in unfair competition by inducing present and former IBM employees to breach their duty of loyalty by revealing trade secrets and other confidential information about IBM's business. . ."

Sure enough, early in 1975, a circuit court overturned the earlier decision and ruled for IBM. It also fined Telex $18.5 Million.

In July 1975, having had one of the largest antitrust cases in history overturned, Telex decided to take its case to the United States Supreme Court. Tensions mounted as the highest court in the land prepared to make its judgment on Telex's petition.

In the 11th hour, both companies decided they had too much to lose if a judgment were found against them, and agreed to a "wash settlement" where Telex would remove its Supreme Court petition and IBM would discharge its counterclaim. So after nearly four years of legal wrangling, both parties dropped all complaints and no money exchanged hands. IBM did, however, soften its policy of allowing third-party devices to be attached to its mainframe computers.

The infancy of open systems computing had begun...

***

Part 4: Murder in Tulsa

Tulsa, Oklahoma. Sunday, May 27, 1981.

It was a sun-filled day at the Southern Hills Country Club. Roger Wheeler had just loaded his golf clubs into the trunk of his car after a casual round of golf with friends, just as he had done a hundred times before.

As he walked towards the driver's door of his car, he probably didn't pay much attention to the dark sedan that silently slid up behind him. Getting into his car, fumbling for his keys and reaching for the ignition, he likely did not notice the two men that left the sedan and were quickly approaching his window.

The next morning, I was among the employees of Telex Computer Products to learn that our CEO Roger Wheeler had been murdered, execution style, with a point-blank shot to the head as he sat in his car with the engine running.

Enter Whitey Bulger and the Winter Hill Gang

For decades, this murder remained unsolved. Over time, however, the events that led up to this heinous act slowly unfolded and eventually caused the unraveling of one of the most notorious mobs of our time: Whitey Bulger and Boston's Winter Hill Gang.

Roger Wheeler was aptly named. He was a free-wheeling Oklahoma businessman. Making his fortune as an entrepreneur, he became one of the wealthiest people in Tulsa during the 60s and 70s.

One of his close friends, Steve Jatras (who succeeded Wheeler as Telex CEO) was a brilliant engineer who saw promise in the burgeoning data storage market and wanted to design a tape drive that could be plugged directly into IBM mainframe computers (see the earlier Telex history in this chapter).

Before Jatras, Wheeler had made a 17% stake in a company called Midwest Instruments, changed the name to Telex and was voted in as CEO. He then asked Jatras to join.

> **Wheeler, himself, was not a technologist:** When asked by a reporter what Telex did, Wheeler responded, "We make widgets, and it's my job to make sure we make money selling those widgets."

Wheeler continued to wheel and deal as Telex CEO, padding his fortune. One of his personal investments was a majority stake in a number of Jai-Alai Frontons in Connecticut and Florida. A sure money-maker, he reckoned. Unfortunately, these establishments were mired in corruption and illegal activities, driven primarily by Bulger's gang.

The mob demand protection money. In his typical wildcat style, Wheeler refused. Wheeler went so far as to testify in an effort to clean up the Jai-Alai gambling industry. A lofty goal indeed, and one that few men would ever attempt. But this was Roger Wheeler, a man among men.

Meanwhile, Bulger's gang was becoming more brazen. Johnny Mortorano--aka "The Cook"--was ordered by Bulger to 'take care' of the Wheeler problem. This would show loyalty and improve his rank in the gang. The Wheeler 'job' was completed on that fateful Sunday in Tulsa.

The Winter Hill Gang Unravels, but Where's Whitey?

As has so often happened in the past, greed and envy became the eventual undoing of the Bulger gang. When John Callahan, fellow Winter Hill Gang member, exposed the details of the Wheeler slaying in 1982, his body was later found in the trunk of a rental car at the Miami airport.

Federal investigators were leaning on their other informants and beginning to put the pieces of this puzzle together. Once they had enough evidence, they moved in to capture Bulger and charge him as the ringleader of the Wheeler execution. Unfortunately, Boston FBI agent John Connolly allegedly tipped off Bulger minutes before the FBI arrived and Whitey disappeared.

Four men were eventually indicted in the Roger Wheeler murder case – two served jailed time, one died before sentencing, and as we now know, Whitey hid in plain sight for 16 years in Santa Monica, California.

Whitey was never convicted for his role in Wheeler's murder. Roger Wheeler was just one of the 19 murder victims listed in Bulger's federal racketeering indictment. Since the feds had an easier time proving other crimes, they focused on those cases and Whitey was eventually found guilty of 11 murders and sentenced to two life terms.

Ironically, according to court testimony from daughter Pam, Wheeler was negotiating to sell all or part of his Jai Alai business:

"Fairly quickly, he was becoming disillusioned with it," Pam Wheeler said. *"It was not performing as he thought it should. ... He liked to do deals."*

***

www.ingramcontent.com/pod-product-compliance
Lightning Source LLC
Chambersburg PA
CBHW071147050326
40689CB00011B/2016